Thelma & Louise

Marita Sturken

bfi Publishing

For my parents
Marie & Bob Sturken

First published in 2000 by the
British Film Institute
21 Stephen Street, London W1P 2LN

The British Film Institute promotes greater
understanding of, and access to, film and
moving image culture in the UK.

Series design by Andrew Barron &
Collis Clements Associates

Typeset in Italian Garamond and Swiss 721BT
by D R Bungay Associates, Burghfield, Berks

Printed in Great Britain by
Norwich Colour Print, Drayton, Norfolk

British Library Cataloguing-in-Publication Data
A catalogue record for this book is available
from the British Library
ISBN 0-85170-809-9

Contents

Acknowledgments

The pleasure of writing this book was aided by the research assistance of Christie Milliken and Courtney Hamilton, the editorial advice of Rob White, and the memories of seeing and discussing *Thelma & Louise* with many girlfriends, in particular Giovanna Di Chiro, Marcy Darnovsky, Patty Wild and Joanna Hefferen. Dana Polan first suggested this book to me, and I am eternally grateful for his attentive advice, support and love. This book is for my parents, who have always been there for me. They think it's a great movie.

Thelma & Louise

In the summer of 1991, *Thelma & Louise* was talked about. It was talked about in the media, in film reviews, on television talk shows, in letters to the editor, over the dinner table, in the local bar, at the water cooler and in the bedroom. It was detested and beloved. Some critics lambasted the film as a violent, male-bashing, superficial story of implausible plot twists. At the same time, *Time* magazine put actresses Susan Sarandon and Geena Davis on its cover with the headline 'Why Thelma and Louise Strikes a Nerve', an image that was quickly converted into a T-shirt reading 'Thelma & Louise Live Forever'.[1] Many film-goers saw the film several times, waiting in anticipation for certain scenes. Academic journals soon began publishing forums on the film, with film scholars criticising and praising the film for its genre play and gender bending. The film, which cost $17.5 million to produce, would go on to make more than $40 million.

It was, more than anything else, a film about which one was supposed to have an opinion. Was it unfair to men? Was it cathartic? Was it encouraging women to emulate bad male behaviour? A distraught reader complained to the *Village Voice*'s mock advice columnist Problem Lady, 'You know you can't go to dinner, or to a party, or even to the corner to buy carrot juice without hordes of people running up to you and saying, "So, *Thelma & Louise*, what about that ending, huh? Was it a

The open road

feminist movie or what the hell was it? Was the violence okay or is it bad for women? What about role models?"[2]

Those cultural products that generate controversy and public debate can be seen, certainly in retrospect, as profoundly, if not poignantly, indicative of particular moments of social change and political upheaval. What was it about this film that so cogently tapped into public fears and desires, that appealed to so many people as the film they had been waiting for, and that was so vehemently dismissed as misguided if not dangerous by others? Was this a crucial turning point in the representation of women, as predicted by some critics, or a regressive cheap shot of reverse sexism?

I still have my Thelma & Louise Live Forever T-shirt, and I remember the stories told by many of my friends that summer of an exhilaration at their first experience of a 'kick ass' women's movie. I remember sitting in audiences where women who I had never heard utter a word at the movies were yelling 'yeah!' at the screen, or hearing about friends saying to some guy hitting on them, 'You'd better watch out, we just went to see *Thelma & Louise!*' That summer, a camping trip I took with two women friends was accompanied by constant playing of the soundtrack as we drove through the deserts and mountains of California. I remember that part of the pleasure in the film was in its being a sleeper hit, an audience-driven success, and an unlikely vehicle for such big issues and debates. In the year that *Thelma & Louise* was released, there was a series of films which addressed issues of women and violence – *La Femme Nikita*, *Sleeping With the Enemy*, *Terminator 2: Judgment Day*, *The Silence of the Lambs* – all of which were, on the face of it, more appropriate texts for public debates about gender. Yet *Thelma & Louise* was by far the most controversial film of its time.

In the controversy that surrounded the film, two crucial issues were debated: the film's relationship to feminism and its depiction of violence. What, these debates asked, was the moral message of the film? *Thelma & Louise* was depicted in many critical reviews as a profoundly violent film. It was called, in a now notorious review in *U.S. News & World Report*, a 'paean to transformative violence … an explicit fascist

'We think you should apologise'

theme wedded to the bleakest form of feminism.'[3] Other reviews said
that it 'justifies armed robbery, manslaughter and chronic drunken
driving as exercises in consciousness raising'[4] and could be 'a recruiting
film for the NRA'.[5] It was accused of being 'degrading to men, with
pathetic stereotypes of testosterone-crazed behaviour'[6] and 'prejudiced
and sexist at its core'.[7] It was defined as an example of 'toxic feminism',[8]
'guerrilla feminism'[9] and labelled a 'betrayal to feminism',[10] 'a sisterhood-
bash-a-thon'.[11] The film was characterised as dangerous, with the
potential to incite young women to lives of crime; as New York columnist
Liz Smith put it, 'I wouldn't send any impressionable young woman I
know to see "Thelma and Louise."'[12] At the same time the film was
defended quite glowingly in *Time* magazine and in extensive articles in
the *New York Times*, which argued 'Lay Off *Thelma & Louise*'.[13]

It would be easy to dismiss much of the debate about feminism and *Thelma & Louise* as a kind of anti-feminist backlash. But it was clearly more complex, in particular because many feminists were opposed to the film. The debate was rather over whose feminism the film represented, and the relationship of women to both anger and violence. In the *Los Angeles Times,* film critic Sheila Benson wrote, 'Call "Thelma & Louise" anything you want but please don't call it feminism, as some writers are already doing. As I understand it, feminism has to do with responsibility, equality, sensitivity, understanding – not revenge, retribution, or sadistic behaviour.'[14] For others, however, the film synthesised feminist principles in important ways: film critic Manohla Dargis wrote, 'In the absence of men, on the road Thelma and Louise create a paradigm of female friendship, produced out of their wilful refusal of the male world and its laws. No matter where their trip finally ends, Thelma and Louise have reinvented sisterhood for the American screen.'[15] Ironically, screenwriter Callie Khouri often responded to criticisms of the film by disavowing the feminist aspects of the film, stating, 'This isn't the story of two women who become feminists; it's the story of two women who become outlaws. They aren't the martyred wife/girlfriend. They aren't the murder victim, the psycho killer, the prostitute: they are outlaws.'[16] She added, rather disingenuously, 'The issues surrounding the film are feminist. But the film itself is not.'[17]

The film was released at a time in the early 90s when the second-wave feminism of the 60s and 70s had emerged from the 80s in a fractured state. Not only had both mainstream and academic feminism been subject to criticisms within feminism, specifically by women of colour and lesbians, about all of the problems of thinking about sisterhood among women who have very different ethnic, class and sexual differences, but the rise of conservatism in the 80s, in particular with Reaganism and Thatcherism in the United States and Great Britain, had also put feminist principles under continuous fire. One year after the release of *Thelma & Louise*, Susan Faludi's book *Backlash* would become tremendously popular in providing a narrative for the turn against feminism during the 80s and 90s. Central to many criticisms of feminism at this time was the stereotypical figure of the male-bashing feminist, who wanted to gain power by taking that of men, and whose potential for violence seemed suddenly to loom large in the public consciousness. The vengeful and spiteful woman, a common figure throughout history, has been tied consistently to women's movements, hence it is no surprise that second-wave feminism has often been accused of fuelling female revenge fantasies. Yet the figure of the vengeful female was brought to a new register in a cultural context in which women were increasingly imagined as having access to guns and the capacity to use them.

Crucial to the debates about feminism in the 80s, as it has been throughout history, was the concern of what it means for women and men to argue that women deserve the same rights and privileges as men, while also arguing that they are different from men. In second-wave feminism in the United States, this argument hinged on what critics saw as the contradictory argument that women needed special legal protection – such as the right to choose whether or not to continue a pregnancy – while they should also have equal legal rights to men. The 80s were a time of conservative attacks on *Roe v. Wade*, the Supreme Court ruling that made abortion legal in the US, and the final rejection of the Equal Rights Amendment (ERA) in the Senate precisely because of conservative campaigns, most notably by Phyllis Schlafly, that convinced a broader public that the ERA would mean unisex bathrooms and the forced conscription of women in the armed services.

What does it mean to be equal yet different? What happens when women do things that are considered to be the province of men only? Much of the criticism of *Thelma & Louise*, especially that of certain feminists, centred on its placing two women within the historically male genre of the outlaw road movie. What is the threat of women feeling free, as one critic noted, 'to behave like – well, men'.[18] Is this feminism, what Sheila Benson calls 'high-toned "Smokey and the Bandit" with a downbeat ending and a woman at the wheel'? Does feminism mean advocating that women have the same right as men to hit the road, take delight in blowing up trucks and break the law? Yet, for others, it was precisely the bold and un-politically correct way in which the film embraced notions of *liberation* that had appeal. In the 90s, the internecine wars of feminism, the public backlash against its basic principles, the disabling academic debates about 'postfeminism', and the quelling of feminist rhetoric made the idea of liberation seem almost quaint if not historical. As Dargis writes,

What kind of feminism are we talking about anyway? *The Second Sex*? bell hooks? Andrea Dworkin? Susie Bright? Granted, *Thelma & Louise* sells a kind of feminism *brut*, inarticulate and inchoate. Yet after more than 10 years of Reagan, Bush, and the murky chimera of post-feminism how many can still speak the language of liberation with any assurance? [19]

Hence, it could be argued that it is precisely because of its crude deployment of the codes of liberation, pure and simple, that *Thelma & Louise* came to stand for many as an icon of feminist film.

The year in which *Thelma & Louise* was released, 1991, was also the year of the Gulf War, a year when large numbers of American women went into combat. Public anxieties about the role of women in war and the change in the gender status quo of the military emerged in the media as a preoccupation with depicting these women as mothers, with regular features displaying women soldiers with their children's pictures on their helmets. In this same time period, the spate of films dealing with women and guns demonstrated the range of cultural ambivalence about women and weapons. *La Femme Nikita*, directed by Luc Besson, tells the story of a young delinquent woman who is recruited and trained by French intelligence into an undercover agent and killer; *Terminator 2: Judgment Day*, directed by James Cameron, has a central role for Linda Hamilton as a tough, gun-wielding, yet maternal, figure who is allied with the (now retooled) good terminator to save her son and the world; *The Silence of the Lambs*, directed by Jonathan Demme, centres on FBI trainee Clarice Starling (Jodie Foster) as a feminist heroine who tracks down and kills a serial killer and saves his young female hostage; *Sleeping With the Enemy* features a young woman (Julia Roberts) who flees and then kills a brutal husband; *V.I. Warshawski* stars Kathleen Turner as a private detective;

and *Mortal Thoughts* is a revenge movie in which Demi Moore is investigated for murdering the abusive husband of a friend.

While these films were written and directed by men, much of the discussion of *Thelma & Louise*'s portrayal of women's relationship to violence centred on the experience of screenwriter Callie Khouri, sometimes called the 'third woman' of *Thelma & Louise*. Khouri won an Academy Award for the screenplay, her first. She is from Kentucky, not that far, geographically speaking, from the small-town context of Arkansas where the film begins. After years working in theatre, as a waitress and at other odd jobs in Nashville and other places, she moved to Los Angeles intending to be an actress. Khouri worked her way from a receptionist to a production co-ordinator to a producer of music videos. She wrote the screenplay at night over a six-month period, looking at a few other scripts to learn format, just to see if she could 'finish it'. At the time that she wrote the script, she states, she was fed up with producing music videos, in particular because of their predominantly sexist narratives: 'In order to get my karma straight about women, I had to write this script. When you become known in the business for producing videos that more often than not have naked women writhing in front of the camera for no reason and to not such interesting music, you eventually have to look at what you're doing.'[20] She states that the primary feeling she wanted in the film was of wanting to bust out: 'I wanted to bust out of my life. ... I was the product of a lot of wasted years and bad relationships and ennui and frustration at not really knowing what I wanted to do.'[21]

Central to Khouri's conception of the script was a desire to present women on the screen who women viewers would identify with, who were familiar yet unpredictable. Khouri's style is tough talking and in response to criticisms of the film, in particular the accusation that it is too violent, she is quick to point to a double standard: 'For [*Thelma & Louise*] to be labeled violent when that same summer *Terminator 2* is being lauded for being so pacifist for shooting all the cops in the knees instead of killing them, it was just mind-boggling.' When asked how she responds to those who call her a male-bashing 'toxic feminist', she retorts:

Kiss my ass. Kiss my ass. I was raised in this society. Let them get their deal worked out about the way women are treated in films before they start hassling me about the way men are treated. There's a whole genre of films known as 'exploitation' based on the degradation of women and a whole bunch of redneck critics extolling its virtues, and until there's a subgenre of women doing the same thing to men in numbers too numerous to count, as is the case with exploitation film, then just shut the fuck up.

It is hard not to see criticisms of *Thelma & Louise* as a violent film as deeply indicative of a double standard on the screen. For this is a film about the consequences of violence, the way in which there is no turning back the clock once one has killed, the remorse that comes from having acted impulsively with a gun. There is one murder in this film, of a man who is a violent rapist. All of the other actions, called 'sadistic' by Benson, are hardly at the level of violence of contemporary drama films, much less action films: a woman robs a grocery store, a policeman is locked in the trunk of his car, a truck is blown up with no one in it.

It could be said, in fact, that fears of the film's impact were patronising to its various audience members. While gossip columnist Liz Smith fretted that she couldn't send a young woman to see the film (presumably for fear that she would run right out and start a career robbing convenience stores), columnist John Leo accused the film of manipulating the audience:

Once we identify with the likable Thelma and Louse and the legitimacy of their complaints about men, we are led step by step to accept the nihilistic and self-destructive values they come to embody. By the time this becomes clear it is very difficult for moviegoers, particularly women, to bail out emotionally and distance themselves from the apocalyptic craziness that the script is hurtling toward.[22]

This accusation – that in establishing an identification with two women who finally have no way out the film is setting up its female viewers to adhere to a nihilistic and self-destructive philosophy – not only ignores the complexity of the film's ending, but also assumes that viewers are easily swayed by what they see on the screen. The viewer might take this literally, these critics seem to imply, in a move that displays a certain contempt for the average movie-goer's capacity to separate story from reality.

As a film about the way in which unlikely and innocent people can be caught in a catch-22 with the law, *Thelma & Louise* asks viewers to consider what they would do if caught in a situation like that. In 1995, two women – one a nurse and suburban mother of two and the other the daughter of a minister – robbed, at gunpoint, several men they met through a dating service in Texas and fled together to Canada. They were instantly dubbed 'Thelma and Louise' by the media.[23] It is perhaps inevitable that the film is thus reduced to the story of two women on a crime spree. That was, indeed, Khouri's initial point of departure when she began to work on her script: 'Two women go on a crime spree.' Yet, crucially, she also asked, 'Why would two women go on a crime spree? Why would *I* go on a crime spree?' Like all outlaw films, *Thelma & Louise* propagates an identification with those who stand outside the law and who do those things that we may secretly desire to do ourselves.

Finally, the accusation that *Thelma & Louise* presents caricatures of men and thus participates in knee-jerk male-bashing was a central aspect of initial debates about the film. The film was described as perpetrating a series of stereotypical men who are caricatures of the worst aspects of masculinity. Even the infinitely sympathetic character of detective Hal Slocombe, played by Harvey Keitel, was seen as a token, an 'Uncle Tom' according to one critic.[24] The lecherous rapist Harlan, the boorish and belittling husband Darryl, the noncommital boyfriend Jimmy, the charming but unreliable thief J.D., the imperious yet ultimately wimpy policeman and the loutish truck driver, for many viewers were humorous commentaries on typical male behaviour, hence recognisable, for many critics they were too easy, too blatantly one-dimensional, hence unrecognisable. Director Ridley Scott has often said that he saw the male characters in the film as comprising various aspects of all men: 'If you look at the film as an allegory and you combine the hitchhiker, the

The men in *Thelma & Louise*

boyfriend, the cop, the husband, the rapist, and the truck driver, you've
pretty well got what approaches one whole male.'[25]

Khouri's script is actually much more sympathetic to many of these
characters than the final film. The character of Hal Slocombe is shown
with his family, asking his wife's advice about whether she would ever
feel compelled to shoot a man (your cousin Eddie, 'because he's an
inconsiderate asshole', she replies). The boyfriend Jimmy is much more
prone to sweetheart language and much quicker to profess his love for
Louise, and the character of Darryl doesn't have quite the same sardonic
bite on the page. Khouri states:

When you read the script you'll see that in *Thelma & Louise*, the male
characters were portrayed in a way that was more caricatured on the screen
than on the page. And that was a decision made by the male director and
the male actors who played them. But that notwithstanding, there are plenty
of truck drivers out there who make obscene gestures to women. There is
not one single gesture in that script that I didn't witness with my own eyes.

The cry of male-bashing, while predictable, was also a source of anger for
the women associated with the film. They often used, as a point of
reference, the recently released Arnold Schwarzenegger film *Total Recall*,
in which, during one well-known scene, Schwarzenegger shoots a woman
in the head and says, in typical deadpan fashion, 'Consider that a
divorce.' Sarandon states, 'I don't hear anyone talking about female-
bashing when Arnold puts a bullet through a woman's head or when the
bulk of Hollywood movies have male characters who are fleshed out and
women characters who are cardboard caricatures.'[26]

That *Thelma & Louise*, a film heralded as the ultimate feminist film
of the 90s, was made by a male director whose reputation had been built
on science fiction action films, such as *Blade Runner* (1982) and *Alien*
(1979), confounded many of the film's critics. It is true that Scott had
created one of the most interesting heroines of science fiction film when
he cast Sigourney Weaver in the role of Ripley in *Alien*, a role originally
written for a man, but he was not known for making 'women's pictures'

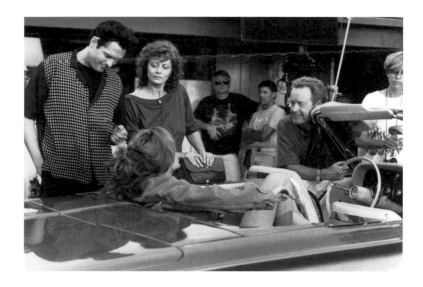

or films based on character. Indeed, much of the sensibility of the film comes from the tension of Scott's direction of the landscape in relation to Khouri's script. Scott tends to describe work on the picture not only as a remarkably easy experience, but also, somewhat unconvincingly, as one in which he let the women have control:

There were three against one – Susan, Geena, and Callie. They were enormously protective of their roles. I'd walk onto the set and they'd wonder what this boy was doing there. … The girls just took over. It's their film, with my slight adjustments. Originally, I was on board as a producer. When I began interviewing other directors about the project, I became so jealous that someone else would be spending time with these fantastic women, I hired myself.[27]

It has been pointed out by many critics that the audiences that were drawn to *Thelma & Louise* were comprised of women and men, and that while the film may have had a particular kind of cathartic pleasure for many women, it was also quite popular with men. 'I'd be a millionaire if I

Ridley Scott on set

had a nickel for every time a guy came over and said, "I was one of the few guys that loved that movie,'" Khouri says. While the image of women audience members yelling in unison at the screen may conjure retrospective pleasure for some, the complexity of the film goes far beyond the simple enjoyment of a kick ass film. Interestingly, many female film critics engaged in a fantasy about the potential of the film to change the behaviour of men on the street, particularly truck drivers, towards women. In *Newsweek*, Laura Shapiro wrote, 'Last week four women who had seen the film were walking down a Chicago street when a truck driver shouted an obscenity at them. Instantly, all four seized imaginary pistols and aimed them at his head. "Thelma and Louise hit Chicago!" yelled one.'[28] And, in *Time* magazine, Margaret Carlson mused, 'next time a woman passes an 18-wheeler and points her finger like a pistol at the tires, the driver might just put his tongue back in his mouth where it belongs.'[29]

If viewing the film prompted this kind of fantasy of empowerment and revenge on the part of many women viewers, the strength of *Thelma & Louise* is that it is not simply about catharsis. The collaborative synthesis of Khouri's script, Scott's direction and the actors' engagement with their roles produced a film that can be seen, in retrospect, to have pushed at broader issues of gender representation, identification, empowerment and the law. When *Thelma & Louise* was released, one critic declared, 'ten years from now it will be seen as a turning point'.[30] Yet it is difficult to say, almost ten years later, that it constituted such a turning point, given that the representation of women in film remains, to this day, deeply problematic. Or, for that matter, that it did anything to change the behaviour of men toward women on the streets or on the road. Perhaps precisely because of this, the film demands our scrutiny.

Genre Bending

It is central to the story of *Thelma & Louise* that the film's female protagonists start out with very different intentions than where they end up. The film's first section is remarkably carefree in tone, playing off the differences of the two women and setting the viewer up for a light-hearted screwball comedy of two women on a weekend away from their dreary lives and unsatisfying relationships. It is crucial to the film's relationship to genre that Thelma and Louise do not set out to become criminals, they become them unintentionally, almost by chance. It is this shift, from screwball comedy to buddy movie to road movie to outlaw movie, that gives the film its hybrid genre status, but also, importantly, makes it a rereading of several classic film genres. As unlikely criminals and outlaws, Thelma and Louise recall and then rescript many iconic heroes of American cinema.

In exploring the film's unlikely status, we could start with the name, *Thelma & Louise*. First of all, the ampersand stands out. This is not a distant coupling with an 'and', Thelma *and* Louise. It is a team, a partnership. This is a title that situates this film in the long line of outlaw teams, paired throughout cinematic history: Bonnie and Clyde, Butch Cassidy and the Sundance Kid. Yet something else is also signalling difference to us in this title: Thelma, an outlaw's name? Louise? These are old-fashioned names, small-town names, with no mystique or charisma, names we are more likely to associate with grandmothers. They sound like the names of women who have not left home, not ventured far from their towns, women who obey the rules. Indeed, they sound more like female comedy teams, like Lucy and Ethel or Laverne and Shirley. These are the names of unintentional outlaws, women who tried to play by the rules but who failed because the rules themselves are not fair.

Thelma & Louise has been situated by numerous film scholars in a wide range of genres, from the fairytale and the screwball comedy to the rape-revenge film and the buddy movie. In deploying many of the conventions of a variety of genres, the film can be seen as both naively and shrewdly playing off these codes and formulas. Primary among its references is the outlaw film, which has a long tradition in American cinema as both westerns and road movies. The outlaw is a central figure in American mythology, with its embrace not only of the idea of the rugged individual but of the notion of the American western frontier as a realm where the 'real' men are those who follow a different law than that of the country. Hence, icons of American history may include the moral and upstanding Abraham Lincoln, but they also include Jesse James, an outlaw in the late nineteenth century whose bank robberies and exploits are central to an idealised history of the American West. The outlaw was mythologised as someone who defied the system (the law, capitalism and the work ethic) for the vicarious pleasure of the constrained and law-abiding citizen who followed his exploits.

In its situation within the landscape of the American West, *Thelma & Louise* can be seen as playing off the outlaw genre's conventions that were most firmly established in the 60s with two films, both star vehicles, *Bonnie and Clyde* (1967), with Warren Beatty and Faye Dunaway, and *Butch Cassidy and the Sundance Kid* (1969), with Paul Newman and Robert Redford. These two films effectively affirmed a 60s version of the genre, which both reiterated its conventions and resituated them within a 60s ideology of liberation. In these films the viewer's identification with the outlaw takes on new ramifications of cultural resistance and defiance of convention.

Thelma & Louise can chart its legacy through these films. *Bonnie and Clyde* is a story not only about the romanticisation of the outlaw but also specifically about the relationship of sexuality and guns. As such, it both affirmed and departed from earlier films of couples on the lam, such as the much-beloved B-movie *Gun Crazy* (1949). The couple express their passion for each other through their guns and crime sprees, yet the consummation of their sexual relationship is the result of their increased media profile: Clyde's impotence ends when Bonnie publishes her poem about them in the newspaper. Yet it is really *Butch Cassidy and the Sundance Kid*, with its mix of crime and screwball humour, that sets the tone of the outlaw film that *Thelma & Louise* will play with.

Butch Cassidy and the Sundance Kid affirms the convention of the outlaw genre of a team of criminals on the lam. The team approach, which it shares with the buddy movie, conventionally establishes a kind of dualism in a film, in which the difference between the two heroes is used for both humorous effect and as an element in their effectiveness as criminals. In *Butch Cassidy*, the Sundance Kid is the expert shot; Cassidy is a lousy gunslinger, but he is the man with the plan. The team aspect of

these films allows for a certain element of screwball comedy, in particular through a teasing kind of banter about skill and plans. In one of *Butch Cassidy*'s most famous scenes, the Sundance Kid is forced to confess that he can't swim while cornered on a cliff with Cassidy over a raging river, prompting a hoot of amusement from Cassidy. Throughout the film, the central comic element involves the two criticising each other for their poor planning or screw-ups.

Thelma & Louise takes this convention and plays it both ways. The film begins by establishing the differences between the two women. Louise is a sardonic waitress, who chides young customers for smoking ('ruins your sex drive') before she lights up in the kitchen, and who gives the air of being world-weary in a small-town kind of way. Thelma putters around her kitchen with tousled hair, constantly taking a half-eaten candy bar out of the freezer and taking a bite before putting it back again. Louise is compulsively neat; she arranges her suitcase into careful piles, puts her shoes in plastic bags and smooths out all wrinkles in her clothes.

Butch and Sundance

Thelma, her hair held high in huge curlers, packs by dumping a whole drawer of underwear into her two suitcases and emptying her entire closet. Her naivety is established through her inability to know what one takes on a trip away – after all, has she ever been away for the weekend before? Louise is tight and orderly, she washes a glass, dries it and folds the towel neatly on the counter. She wears her hair in a prim scarf. Thelma is barely contained chaos.

Louise, tightly wound and disappointed in life; Thelma, naive and messy. The film begins by cross-cutting these packing scenes between the two to establish their pairing. Louise is the older, wiser teacher. Thelma is the younger, sheltered one. Louise brings the car, Thelma brings the gun.

The differences between Thelma and Louise

Yet, it is the car that shows Louise is not content with the confines of her neatly organised apartment. The car, a green 1966 Thunderbird convertible, is the height of impracticality, a veritable road car meant to put its driver on display. (The production actually used five Thunderbirds in total.) Louise's attachment to the car is played out much more in the script. At one point, Thelma says to her, 'You care more about that car than you do about most people.' She replies, 'Most people just cause me trouble, but that car always gets me out of it.' In the final film, she is protective of the car, yelling at a few errant cows on a dirt road, 'Don't dent my car!' The car is Louise's one concession to indulgence, and ultimately its conspicuousness is crucial to the story's end. Yet the film begins with Louise and her car as a contradiction in terms; she drives a convertible with the top down, but always with a neat scarf wrapped around her head to keep her hair tidy while doing so.

While *Thelma & Louise* delineates these characters at its beginning, the film's most important progression has to do with how they change roles within their pairing. For the first section of the film, Thelma is childish and impulsive, often imitating a whining puppy when asking Louise, the parental figure, to stop at the bar or to pick up the hitchhiker. However, once Louise begins to truly despair, after J.D. the hitchhiker has stolen her $6,500 – money that she spent years scrupulously saving and which she was counting on to get them to Mexico – Thelma is transformed into a new person. Whereas before she was so unreliable that when counting her money she accidently lets twenty dollars fly out the window, she now takes charge, gets Louise on the road and robs a convenience store to get them money. This scene is pivotal in the shift in power between Louise and Thelma. Says Davis, 'We were best friends, but in a sense we're just discovering this relationship. Louise has never fallen apart before. It's pretty profound to see this happen. But I realize that one of us has to not fall apart, so this is the scene where I start taking control.'[31] One of the criticisms of this scene is that it appears to establish Thelma as transformed by her first pleasurable sexual experience (with J.D.), a kind of orgasmic life change. Yet the film has established Louise, rather than Darryl or J.D., as the central relationship of Thelma's life, and this scene makes clear that, for Thelma, Louise's collapse is a much more transformative event.

Thelma's transformation begins at first by her borrowing the words of others. She repeats Louise's line when she tells off her husband Darryl on the phone, 'You're my husband, not my father,' and she imitates J.D.'s technique as a polite robber to the word. Yet, as the film progresses, she makes this personality more individually her own. Geena Davis states, 'I just really loved the character and [thought] the huge changes that she goes through in the movie would be challenging to pull off. I've never come across a character that had such a giant arc.'[32] By the end of the film, Thelma is the one who speaks with the most confidence, who reminds Louise why they fled, who seems to see clearly their destiny and who suggests that they continue their journey out over the cliff.

In outlaw films, there are other characters who enter into the narrative and affect it in certain ways, but who must by necessity drop out of the picture in order for the primary relationship of the team to be affirmed. In *Butch Cassidy and the Sundance Kid*, the character of Etta Place, played by Katharine Ross, is an essential third person, who is Sundance's lover and shares her affection with Cassidy, yet it is crucial that she chooses to leave the pair when their doom seems imminent. In *Thelma & Louise*, various men enter into the narrative, yet each must leave in a certain sense before the ending. Jimmy, Louise's boyfriend, helps them by bringing the money, but Louise refuses not only to let him

J.D. teaching Thelma the tricks of polite robbery

come along but also to tell him what happened. J.D. changes their fate by stealing the same money, but he also teaches Thelma the basics of small-time robbery, which allows them to continue forward. Hal Slocombe, the amiable detective, wants to connect with the women, to understand them, to be their empathetic paternal figure, but letting him closer proves to be fatal. It is crucial to the narrative that these men can affect the action of the women, if not make it veer sharply, but they are ultimately dispensable in the story.

One of the features of an outlaw film is that the heroes are understood to be on journeys toward their fate and that they are stripped of many possessions along the way. In *Butch Cassidy and the Sundance Kid*, the men gradually lose all of their most important possessions as they attempt to escape a relentless posse always on the horizon (with their constant refrain as a motif throughout the film, 'Who are those guys?'). First, they lose the rest of their gang in a shoot-out, then they set their horses loose in an attempt to trick the posse, they lose their hats when they jump off the cliff, their woman leaves them in Bolivia, and finally they are left with only their guns. The outlaw heroes are often reduced to the essentials of survival and rendered elemental, alone in the wilderness. In an interesting twist on this, Thelma and Louise go through the process of losing many things, but they gain others simultaneously. Louise loses her money, presumably her job and her boyfriend, but she holds onto her car. She trades her jewellery, including an engagement

Louise trades her jewellery for a new hat and identity

ring, for an old man's cowboy hat, her sunglasses for the policeman's, and her tight headscarf for a bandana around her neck. Thelma goes from frilly dresses to jeans and a T-shirt with a skull and the line 'Driving My Life Away' on it, leaves her wedding ring behind in the motel, and finally takes the ratty baseball cap from the truck driver during a final spin around him after they have blown up his truck. So, while they lose the accoutrements of traditional femininity over the course of the film, they also take as their own several signifiers of masculinity and the road.

The story of the American outlaw is a story about encroaching modernity. In *Butch Cassidy and the Sundance Kid*, the outlaws are faced with the seemingly inevitable movement of technological progress, represented by trains and increased techniques of law enforcement. Mechanisation is part of what both defines and destroys these outlaws. Cassidy and Sundance rob trains, but their world is one of horses and the open range. Bonnie and Clyde are dependent on cars for their getaways and even take on gang member C.W. precisely because he can repair them. Yet these characters are also about the myths of modernity and the access to money that it provides through such modern institutions as banks. In both films, photographs are central to how the outlaws define themselves and to their media reputations. Cassidy and Sundance pose for pictures on their travels, while Bonnie and Clyde constantly photograph not only each other and their gang, posing with their guns, but some of their victims as well. Similarly, Louise holds up a Polaroid camera as she and Thelma take off on their journey, to photograph themselves – a photograph that poignantly flies out of the back of the convertible when it makes its final drive off the cliff. Yet, whereas the earlier outlaw couples flirt with the publicity they have generated, and Bonnie and Clyde clearly thrive on it, Thelma and Louise are desperate to be anonymous. As Louise says when contemplating their fate, 'I don't want to end up on the damn Geraldo show.' Thelma and Louise are confronted with the machine world of modernity constantly in their journey, as their paths are constantly crossed by trucks, planes and, finally, helicopters. Indeed, it is the technology of surveillance that ultimately defines Thelma as a robber. Yet, these women are not, like the

male heroes of the 60s, on a journey of nostalgia. Their journey is inexorably away from the past.

In placing two women in the role of outlaws *Thelma & Louise* recasts, in many ways, the outlaw genre. It is not the first film to do so. French director Alain Tanner's 1981 *Messidor* is about two young women who, wandering and hitchhiking aimlessly in the Alps, end up killing a rapist, taking an army officer's gun, stealing food from stores and finally committing murder. And the Roger Corman B-movie, *The Great Texas Dynamite Chase* (1977), features two women who rob banks, seduce men, show lots of flesh and finally escape to South America. However, through its soft-porn plot, the film is more of a male fantasy than a female one. While *Messidor* might seem to share some similarities with *Thelma & Louise* in its slow realism and dark cast, it is almost its opposite in terms of tone and cinematic style.

The fact that Thelma and Louise are accidental outlaws, who happen into crime and then spend the rest of the film trying to escape the law, is crucial to the film's reworking of the genre. What kind of crimes are these? Within the context of this story, they are crimes of impulse that become

Photographing themselves

crimes of necessity. Louise kills the rapist because he is unremorseful, Thelma robs the store because they need money to escape to Mexico, they lock the policeman in the trunk of his patrol car because otherwise he will report them and, finally, with necessity no longer the motivation, they blow up the truck because the driver has been sexist and crude.

If nothing else, this list demonstrates the extent to which issues of traditional female demeanour are central to the film's retooling of the outlaw film. When women become unlikely outlaws, the film seems to be saying, they still retain certain codes about what constitutes decent human behaviour. Thelma first explores the role of renegade by practising smoking in the mirror ('I'm Louise') and then purchasing only small airline-size bottles of Wild Turkey ('Ma'am, you sure you wouldn't rather have a large economy size?'). The women blow up the trucker's truck, not simply because he has acted toward them in a crude and lecherous manner, but because he refuses to apologise for his behaviour. Indeed, Louise kills Harlan not because of what he did, but because of what he said.

This gender bending of the outlaw genre is also a joke on the genre itself. Thelma, who confesses that she learned to shoot 'off the TV', turns out to be a great shot. Two improbable women, with no experience in evading the law, end up leading the police on a long chase, effectively keeping them at bay until the landscape hems them in. If they can do it, the film seems to say, then what's the big deal?

'I'm Louise'

Contentions of Space: The Domestic and the Frontier

Thelma & Louise is a film about space, both the wide open space of the American West and the confining interior space of the home. The film opens with a shot of a two-lane road that leads out towards a western landscape, slowly fading from black and white into colour, a road that reappears at the end of the film just before the women drive into the canyon. The film thus establishes early on the importance of both the road and the landscape to its story. Yet, it moves very quickly from that wide open space to the cramped interiors of Louise's restaurant and Thelma's dark house. Similarly, the film begins in the nondescript small-town atmosphere of Arkansas, a state more closely associated with the South than the West, before moving into a more expansive countryside.

Director Ridley Scott originally intended to shoot the film in Arkansas, Oklahoma and Arizona, as defined in the story by the women's Texas-avoiding journey toward Mexico, but after driving the route, he decided that many of the locales were easier to shoot, and identical in landscape and tone, to California. Hence, the majority of the film was shot within a few hours of Los Angeles, with Tarzana, California standing in for Arkansas, a restaurant in the San Fernando Valley as Louise's restaurant, a saloon in Long Beach as the Silver Bullet cowboy bar (where local dancer extras spontaneously did the scene of line dancing), and the farmland and oil rigs surrounding Bakersfield directly north of

The opening shot of the film, which returns towards its end

Los Angeles as the landscape of Oklahoma. Most of the scenes of New Mexico and Arizona were shot in Utah and Western Colorado.

As a British film-maker, Scott brought to the film a particular kind of European fascination with the American West: 'There are a lot of things that Americans live with that they never really see, because they are such a part of their culture. ... As an "outsider", however, I can drive around the desert Southwest and get excited about miles and miles of telephone poles – telephone poles that the average American might take for granted.'[33] He expresses his great love of the expanse of the Bakersfield landscape, of farms with no walls or fences, 'to give a sense of being in the middle of this great land mass you call United States of America'. In fact, the production spent some time searching for a few locales where telephone poles still existed along long western roads, since most of them are now gone. This desire to represent the West of open space and traditional technology is a nostalgia fed, of course, by classic Hollywood films, however Scott was also interested in the American landscape of oil rigs, cheap motels next to the highway and nondescript roadside coffee houses. This is not a road populated by McDonald's and Burger King, but rather the landscape of the side roads off the interstate that hark back to a different era of the road. As Scott has stated, 'I felt it was better to lean to the vanishing face of America, which is Route 66, rather than the new face of America, which is malls and concrete strips.'[34] The romance of this landscape is heightened by the steel guitar soundtrack that wails in the background as the women drive further and was created by another European, German composer Hans Zimmer.

The film moves from this generic western landscape to its most romantic iconic representation, the canyon, first in Canyonlands – specifically in Moab, Utah – and then at the lower end of the Grand Canyon in Arizona. While not quite as favoured a movie locale as Monument Valley, Moab has been the site of many John Ford westerns, plenty of science fiction adventures and such diverse films as *Easy Rider* and *Indiana Jones and the Last Crusade*. When Louise stops the car on their last night, just as the early morning sky is beginning to get light, and stands among the high cliffs and rock formations, the desert is inscribed as a kind of timeless locale for such reflection (set to Marianne Faithful's song, 'The Ballad of Lucy Jordan', about a housewife going crazy as she realises 'she'd never ride through Paris in a sports car with the warm wind in her hair'). At this point, the women are tanned and rugged-looking, seeming to fit fully within the landscape. Scott lit the cliffs of Moab up like a movie set, which only makes them look more surreal and mystical.

While it could be said that the story of *Thelma & Louise* definitely belongs to Callie Khouri and actors Davis and Sarandon, the visual look of the film is all Scott's. The open horizons of the film give it a kind of epic sweep that heightens the story itself. Scott is responsible for the fact that as the two women drive on the open road, their pathway is constantly interrupted by signifiers of the road as male territory. A street-cleaner sprays them with water, huge trucks cut them off, a motorcyclist roars past just as they approach a stop sign, a noisy freight train rushes past, a plane flies low overhead, a bulldozer crosses in front of them and a muscleman lifts weights at a gas station. They are even surrounded at one point by a herd of cattle and a few cowboys, stymied, as it were, in Marlboro country. Scott brought much of this sensibility to the script, but he also improvised some of it on the spot, for example, one day paying the pilot of a crop-duster plane $200 to fly over a few times and then take the camera up in the plane. The result is a disarming shot, as the camera turns to fly over the car and someone's shirt sleeve flaps in the wind. He also added the incongruous black bicycle rider who arrives, smoking a joint, to find the policeman locked in his trunk, reduced from his former power to poking his wimpy finger out of a hole Thelma shot in the trunk.

Scott depicts the western road as the territory of men and machines, in which women are transgressing when they are driving, rather than working as store clerks, waitresses or prostitutes. Yet he presents the road not as a simple escape from the past, but as a series of obstacles that ultimately signal the film's final obstacle – the helicopter that confronts them, rising up from behind the cliff. The road, we must understand, is never entirely open to the women. On location at the time, Sarandon described the experience of shooting the film as a kind of strenuous road trip in itself:

The western landscape of men, horses and coffee shops

We meet Ridley in a desolate area and get in a car and drive eight hours in the blistering sun. Finally we just surrender to his judgment. I mean, you will read a scene that in the script seems straightforward, but then suddenly it is happening with a screaming Mack truck on either side of you. ... we've got this strange effect of having a women's *Odd Couple* traffic into *Mad Max* country.[35]

Scott's techniques as a director come from a long background in directing commercials before doing film. He works quickly, prefers that his actors not rehearse and often shoots scenes using two cameras at once. These are strategies, according to Scott, to save the actors and capture a spontaneity on film. He states, 'I think there's nothing worse than when you rehearse, rehearse until every ounce of adrenalin is gone. That's when you end up with forty takes trying to make it look spontaneous. If we did five or six takes, it was a lot.'[36]

The film's establishment of the road as a site of liberation for the women, an escape from both their dreary lives and the law, situates it quite firmly within the genre of the road movie. The road movie, which is a particularly postwar American genre, reached its height in the 60s and 70s, with, in addition to outlaw films *Bonnie and Clyde* and *Butch Cassidy and the Sundance Kid*, such films as *Easy Rider* (1969), *Badlands* (1973) and *Kings of the Road* (1976), a German film by Wim Wenders that is essentially a road movie in homage to cinema.

The classic road movie was about male privilege, the right to hit the road without worrying about the kids or a destination. Women were not the protagonists of road movies, they were more often than not what the men were running away from. They were not awarded the privilege of travel. It is not incidental that Thelma, who has never gone away without her husband, says, 'I always wanted to travel, I just never got the opportunity' (or that he drives a fancy red Corvette and she has a Honda that, as she puts it, barely makes it down the driveway). Timothy Corrigan defines the classic road movie as having four defining features: a breakdown of the family unit, a context in which events are acted upon characters and obstacles are constantly being presented in the way, a protagonist who is readily identified with their means of transportation, be it an automobile or

Mad Max country

a motorcycle, and a focus on men in the absence of women.[37] The road movie is about the automobile as an expression of freedom and individuality, in which stopping on the road brings problems and vulnerability. Since the 60s, in the era of *Easy Rider* (1969), the road movie has increasingly portrayed those who are outside of society for whom the road represents a temporary reprieve from social conventions and the law.

In more recent years, road movies have charted the journeys of many different kinds of protagonists, including those to whom the road was not previously hospitable. Many critics have credited *Thelma & Louise* with reviving the genre and opening it up to new kinds of identities:

After *Thelma & Louise*, Hollywood films began to recognize again the increasing hospitality of the road to the marginalized and alienated – not only women (*Leaving Normal*), but also gays (*My Own Private Idaho, The Living End, To Wong Foo, Thanks for Everything! Julie Newmar*), lesbians (*Boys on the Side, Even Cowgirls Get the Blues*), and people of color (*Get on the Bus, Fled, Powwow Highway*) – and to renew the road's historical currency.[38]

Thelma and Louise follow the tradition of the road movie protagonists in that they are most happy and free while moving. Almost every time they stop, they get into trouble: Thelma almost gets raped and Louise kills a man; they pick up J.D., who steals their money; and they call home in an increasingly tangled web with the police. Yet, the film is also constantly reiterating a duality of space. The open road of the two women is contrasted throughout the film with the small-town and domestic interiors they left behind. In other words, the film does a reversal on the traditional theme in which men ride through the landscape which is coded as woman/nature. While Thelma and Louise are in motion and on the run, the primary men in the film are stationary and house bound. Arkansas detective Hal Slocombe and the FBI men gather at Thelma's house with Darryl to wait for the women to make contact. In the dark, unappealing interior of the home, they must deal with each other until

the women give them something to go on (this is relatively implausible in terms of how police work, but it provides a crucial juxtaposition in the film). The domestic space is one that the men inhabit awkwardly. The first time that Thelma calls, Darryl is home watching a football game, surrounded by empty beer cans, which clearly shows it was Thelma's job to clean up for him. He yells at her – 'Have you lost your mind? Is that it? Now, I leave for work and you take complete leave of your senses?' – and then covers the phone while he watches in frustration as his team fumbles the ball. When the police arrive, the house has fallen into further disarray, as Darryl mistakenly steps on a pizza strewn on the floor. Yet, later, like a good housewife, he asks them to wipe their feet.

The women are on the wide open road while the men are stuck in domestic space

Darryl playing housewife and detective

The men are forced in this context to participate in codes of female behaviour. While the women's identities at the beginning of the film were defined by them *waiting on* people, Thelma as a housewife and Louise as a waitress, the men are now forced to *wait for* them. Now, the men have to clean off the tables, they eat out of boredom and, in the codes of feminine behaviour, they wait for the phone to ring (they also read porno magazines). We even see them watching an old Cary Grant film on television, which Darryl mischievously switches to a sports game before sheepishly changing it back. Whereas the women are constantly driving into the sun, the men either slog through rain or sit in darkened rooms. Hence, while the film began by cross-cutting between the two women, once they are on the road it cross-cuts between the women and the men who are left behind, trying to catch them and, finally, waiting for their call.

The humour of these scenes is driven by the caricature of manhood that Darryl presents, both in his belittling treatment of Thelma, established quite early in the film, and his pathetic attempt to play at lawman with the detectives. Advised by the FBI man Max to talk sweetly to Thelma if she calls, because 'women love that shit', Darryl puts on such a fake voice that the women know immediately that the police are there. Playing detective, Darryl tries again, casually asking Louise, 'Hey, where are you girls, anyway?' This is the only scene in which we are asked to feel sympathy for Darryl, played by Christopher McDonald (who is credited by Scott with amping up the humour and creating new dialogue in his scenes), when, as the police close in, we see him sitting alone in tears, defeated and confused.

The contrast of the domestic space of the men and the open space of the women on the road sets the stage for what could be understood as the contradictory discursive space established in the film between men and women. Put simply, the male and female characters of the film do not have the same understanding of words or ways of expressing themselves. Indeed, they speak past each other, as if they are sometimes speaking different languages. Hence, the film establishes not only the ways in which physical space is gendered, and then recoded, but also how space, knowledge and human nature are understood quite differently by men and women.

How, for instance, do men and women interpret the actions and words of each other? The film establishes quite early on that men and women, even when on intimate terms, often don't occupy the same discursive space. In Thelma and Darryl's first exchange, she yells at him from the kitchen to make sure he is not listening in on her phone conversation with Louise ('Goddamnit, Thelma, don't holler like that!') and then each time she attempts to ask him about going away for the weekend, she loses her courage and says something else instead ('You want anything special for dinner?'). Each one is effectively lying to the other in ways that are transparent to the viewer, as Thelma thinks it 'funny' that Darryl has to work on a Friday night selling carpets, a clear hint that she is on to the fact that he is probably doing something else, and he dismisses this as her naivety ('Well then, it's a good thing you're not regional manager and I am'). Later, the mutual misunderstanding and misrecognition between Thelma and Darryl is made clear when he is asked by Hal if he is 'close' to Thelma, and he replies, 'I love Thelma,' and then pauses, 'Yeah, I guess, I mean I'm about as close as I can be to a nutcase like that.'

As the women are transformed through the series of events in the film, they become even more indecipherable to the men in their lives. Jimmy's attention to Louise, which has always been a sore point in their

'It's a good thing that you're not regional manager and I am'

relationship, is heightened when he sees that she is moving away from him. Yet, even then, he and Louise cannot speak the same language. When Louise asks Jimmy if he loves her, the pause at the other end of the line is interminable. He screws up his face, takes a puff of his cigarette and finally manages to half-heartedly eke out the word, 'Yeah'. This is the moment when Louise irrevocably turns away from Jimmy. He has no idea that after that moment roses, professions of love and even an engagement ring cannot make up for that pause and the hesitation and ambivalence it evoked. Yet, Jimmy follows Louise even though, as he is quick to mention, he 'hates to fly'. When he actually does begin to speak the way Louise would like, she wonders if he has taken a 'pill that makes you say all the right stuff', and he replies, 'Yeah, I'm choking on it.' It is thus understood in the film that men and women do not normally speak the other's language.

It is interesting to note that Khouri's script is much kinder to Jimmy, who is quick to profess his love to Louise. But Michael Madsen, who plays Jimmy, and Sarandon, who rewrote a scene between the two, created a character who was much more in the throes of ambivalence. In the original script, Louise and Jimmy have a very tender scene in the motel in which they profess their love and act out a fake marriage ceremony in which they vow 'to have and to hold for the rest of the night, through richness and poorness and breakfast at the coffee shop until your plane leaves or it gets light, whichever comes first'. However, Sarandon felt that it was only in the script as a counterpoint to Thelma's love scene with J.D., and she and her partner Tim Robbins rewrote it.[39] In the original script, this scene operates to give a sense of hope to Louise's relationship to Jimmy well into the film.

Can men and women really know each other? Much of the catharsis of *Thelma & Louise* for audiences is the way in which it captures the tensions that create both difficulty and attraction between men and women. In this sense, the film embraces one of the fundamental aspects of the buddy film, which is that men understand each other better than they understand their women. The primary relationship in this film is between two women, who understand each

'Yeah, I'm choking on it'

other's ways of being in the world more than their men (Louise, for instance, has always appreciated that Thelma was a 'little crazy'). The buddy relationship has always been an affirmation of friendship in contrast to the complexities of intimate relationships between men and women.

During their journey, the women encounter many men who symbolise the extremes of how women and men misunderstand each other. The most crude example is the trucker, who makes lewd gestures at them while driving by, gestures which they later question him on ('What's that supposed to mean, exactly?'). They, of course, make no sense to him. Here are two women driving a convertible, they must, he thinks, be available. When he stops his truck at their behest, he takes off his wedding ring and grabs a couple of condoms, and then asks them, 'You girls about ready to get serious?' The humour of the miscommunication lies precisely in his and their different interpretations of what it means to 'get serious'.

The one male character in the film who attempts to bridge the different discursive spaces of men and women is Hal, whose sensitivity to what the women are going through seems just a tad too unrealistic. He is genuinely concerned about them, if not sympathetic to their plight, but he also speaks to them like they are children ('Be careful with that gun. … You girls are in some hot water'). Hal is a man of another sort, a well-intentioned, earnest man who presumes that he can know what the women are thinking. Yet he is often wrong. For instance, he presumes that Thelma's packing technique is evidence not of a scattered style and naivety about what to take, but of an intention to stay away for a long time. When Hal first begins to investigate the women, he goes to Louise's apartment and, since he has no warrant, lets himself in with the help of a credit card. He wanders through her space, noting the excessive cleanliness and looking at the photographs. The scene presents a fine line between curiosity and invasiveness, and it allows Hal to feel that he has been privy to the private Louise and her secrets.

In the codes of gender difference established in the film, Hal's belief that he can, for instance, really 'know' Louise ('I swear Louise, I almost feel like I know you') is misguided. She rebuffs him ('Well, you don't'), but he has another one of her secrets ('I know what's making you run. I know what happened to you in Texas'). Hal, the investigator, has got closer than Louise has let anyone, including Thelma, get to her personal story. His statement catches her by surprise and she pauses, stunned, until Thelma reaches up and calmly presses down the lever to hang up the phone ('Come on Louise. Don't blow it'). That conversation, in which Hal's knowledge of her keeps her on the phone, is what ultimately leads to the women's location being discovered by the police. In that sense, Hal could be seen as the women's worst enemy, because in his desire to understand them and his capacity to seduce Louise into talking, to almost making her believe that his sympathy can help them, he manages to 'catch' them.

Ultimately, of course, Hal's role is as a policeman and this creates a central narrative in the film about expertise and criminal knowledge. To whom is expertise awarded when men and women disagree? Crucial to the film's engagement with this question is Louise's role as a waitress. The film establishes early on that one of the jobs of a waitress is not simply to wait on people but to interpret their behaviour. Louise sizes up her customers, gives them some advice, begrudgingly attends to their requests and views the world in a weary, I've-heard-it-all-before manner. The waitress is the quintessential working-class female profession, a job in which women are meant to be efficient, maternal and invisible.

'Come on Louise. Don't blow it'

Louise's job designates her as both downtrodden and knowing, particularly compared to Thelma, who has been kept at home, catering to her one customer, Darryl, and who thinks that waiting tables has made Louise jaded. It also creates a connection between her and the other waitresses in the film. When Thelma and Louise stop by the fateful Silver Bullet bar for a drink, Lena, the waitress, immediately bonds with Louise as she tries to keep Harlan from harassing them. Catching Harlan making moves on the women, Lena makes knowing eye contact with Louise as she says, 'It's a good thing they're not all as friendly as you.' Thelma's naivety here, when she babbles to Harlan about why they're taking off for the weekend, is contrasted with the two waitresses, who know a creep when they see one.

After the shooting, when Thelma and Louise have fled, the interpretation of the event becomes a flirtatious contention between Hal and Lena. She is clear in her assessment that 'neither one of them was the type to pull something like this'. However, Hal is now on the job, and the realm of knowledge has changed. The feminine knowledge of the waitress, a version of female intuition, is negated by the professional, methodical knowledge of the law:

HAL: Well, you're not exactly an expert witness, but what makes you so sure?

LENA: If waitin' tables in a bar don't make you an expert on human nature,

Lena responds to Harlan's moves on Thelma

then nothin' will. I could've told you Harlan Puckett would end up buyin' it in a parkin' lot. I'm just surprised it didn't happen sooner than this.

HAL: Who do you think did it?

LENA: Has anybody asked his wife? She's the one I hope did it.

HAL: Lena, do you have any ideas or don't ya?

LENA: Well, if I had to guess, I'd say it was either some ol' gal, or some ol' gal's husband. But it wasn't either one of those two. The smaller one, the one with the tidy hairdo, she left me a huge tip.

The criteria for Lena's evaluation is clear. This guy had it coming; in fact, in her eyes, there is hardly a crime worth pursuing here. And she is correct in her assumption that 'neither of those two was the murdering type'.

In *Thelma & Louise*, men and women speak past each other and misinterpret each other's actions with fatal consequences. When Thelma enjoys dancing, Harlan interprets her as being sexually available. When he is caught trying to rape her, he explains, 'We were just havin' a little fun,' to which Louise replies, 'Looks like you've got a real fucked-up idea of fun.' Hence, at crucial moments, the film establishes the tensions and the violence between men and women in explicitly linguistic terms. When Louise comes upon Harlan trying to rape Thelma, the power dynamics are established through the tight frame of the shot. Harlan has gone from cajoling ('I won't hurt you') to brutal rage, hitting Thelma and tearing off her clothes. As we see Harlan's face, distorted with anger since Thelma has hit him back, we first hear Louise off screen, saying 'let her go'. When he tells her to 'get the fuck out of here', a tight shot reveals only the gun entering into the frame and poking him in the back of the neck. Words have failed, but the gun won't. The gun, among other things, allows Louise the power to speak and to reinterpret Harlan's behaviour: 'In the future, when a woman's crying like that, she isn't having any fun.' And it is words, more than actions, that prompt Louise to pull the trigger. She doesn't kill Harlan because he tried to rape Thelma. They have already decided to walk away. She kills him because he is defiantly unremorseful. He calls after them, 'Bitch. I should have gone ahead and fucked her.' When Louise responds in shock, he is confident and arrogant, never

'I'm not going to hurt you'
'Well, you're not exactly an expert witness'

believing she will shoot: 'I said "suck my cock".' This is the moment when she steps forward, aims and fires, hitting him cleanly in the heart (Louise is a good shot). But she is not done with him; her anger is so palpable, she needs the last word, as she leans over his limp frame and whispers hoarsely, 'You watch your mouth, buddy.'

Given the lightness of the film until this scene, Louise's pulling of the trigger is a shock. Not only is Harlan not expecting it, the audience is also unprepared for this shift in tone. Just as the lives of the characters are changed irrevocably in this moment, the film is too. Any humour that follows this scene, which occurs twenty minutes into the film, is tempered by the shock of this scene, which makes any kind of simple

The gun gives Louise the power to stop Harlan
'You watch your mouth, buddy'

outcome of the story impossible. Until this scene, it is possible that the women could have gotten in a bit of trouble, pissed off a few men and gone home. Now that the law has been broken, there is no turning back. In the transformation that takes place in that moment, when the women first break the law by killing a man and leaving the scene of the crime, they literally become outlaws, and it becomes the job of the men pursuing them to try to understand their behaviour.

Girls, Guns and the Law

How does the law come to 'know' a suspect and what happens to the law when a woman breaks it? Whereas Hal has used his prerogative as a detective to snoop around Louise's house and dig up her old files, he cannot be said, in her terms, to know her. To know someone in legal terms is to know them through technology and certain legal codes of description. *Thelma & Louise* underscores again and again that the system does not quite know what to do with women who break the law. They produce a certain kind of mystification and lots of polite astonishment: how can they do that? As Max, the FBI man, remarks, 'The one thing I can't figure out is whether these girls are real smart or just real, real lucky.'

As the film progresses, and the men get closer to finding out where the women are, it is technology that allows them to do so. When Hal's

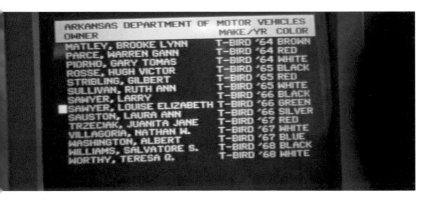

The apparatus of the law

boss first suggests that they should 'let the Bureau in on this', we hear it as a voice over the two women driving, conveying the beginning of the law's technological reach upon them. Hal finds Louise by searching through a data base of cars bearing a similar description. The technology of telephone-call tracing allows the FBI to find the women's last location on the road, and a helicopter enables them to fly in and confront them. The technological gaze of the law is most obvious in the scene when Thelma robs the convenience store. It is crucial to this scene that the audience first remains outside in the car with Louise. She is deeply depressed about the loss of the money that J.D. stole; she looks at herself unhappily in the mirror, makes an attempt to put on some lipstick and then gives up and throws it in the dirt. Two older women are sitting in a storefront window and watch her with muted curiosity. Louise stares back, perhaps contemplating her own future or the future she would have had prior to the recent series of events. At this moment, Thelma comes running towards the car, shouting, 'Drive, Louise, drive, drive, drive the car.' (It is most likely because the two older women were added during location shooting that we have no reaction shot from them as Thelma and Louise drive quickly away.)

The audience participates in Louise's surprise at Thelma's actions, as she looks stunned when Thelma shows her the wads of cash she now has in hand. (This is repeated in the later scene when Thelma holds her

Louise throwing away her lipstick

gun on the policeman and then orders him into the trunk of his patrol
car, as Louise watches her with an expression of surprise and awe.)
Yet, at the moment when Louise asks, 'How d'you? I mean, what
did you say?', we see not Thelma's explanation but the videotape from
the store's surveillance camera. This scene marks a movement forward by
the law towards taking over the space of the road occupied by the
women. Sitting in a dark room, expressing disbelief, the men are shocked
('Jesus Christ', 'Good God', 'My Lord'). The black-and-white video
image defines Thelma's action as a crime – she has entered into the
apparatus of the law. This shift in image, which was part of Khouri's
original script, plays down the potential comedic aspects of this scene. If
it had been shot in a conventional manner, this scene would have been
much more about the comedy of Thelma imitating J.D.'s polite style of
robbing people; instead, it is focused on the stunned reaction of Louise
and the men, a shock that the audience is intended to share in, since we
have been given no hint that Thelma was planning or even capable of
this.

As unlikely outlaws, the two women, in particular Thelma, take to
their new role both with a relish and a particular sense of social codes. In
a certain sense, they have to learn to be outlaws, especially Thelma. She
foils their plans in many ways when she tells J.D. that if he ever goes to
Mexico, he should look them up. Louise, whose sense of caution and
past experiences with the law make her better at being on the run, is
frustrated with Thelma's lack of reserve. She cautions her, 'Thelma, you

Thelma's robbery on the surveillance tape

just got to stop talkin' to people. You've got to stop being so open! We're fugitives now. Let's start behaving that way!' Yet, it is at Louise's instigation that they continue to 'call home'. At first, this is a way to check whether or not the police are on to them. But later, it seems almost to be a reflex, with enormous consequences for their fate, as if they are simply following the social rule that what you do when you are on the road is call home. (It is worth noting that after the murder they both call their respective men, neither of whom are home.)

They may be breaking some laws, but others must be strenuously followed. Just after Thelma has committed the crime of robbing a store at gunpoint, Louise chides her, 'Thelma, don't you litter!' Indeed, never have two outlaws apologised so much when doing things like putting a policeman in the trunk of his car ('Officer, I am so sorry about this. Would you let go of that [radio]? Now, I really, really apologize, but would you put your hands on that steering wheel?'). These codes of politeness are also an essential element in their dealings with the men they encounter on their route, who they punish not so much for their actions as for their rudeness. One of Thelma's main arguments to Louise about why they should give J.D. a ride is that he is polite, which he is, addressing them as 'Miss Thelma' and 'Miss Louise'. Further, they shoot up the truck driver's massive vehicle after chiding him, 'We think you should apologize' – clearly apologising would have saved his truck (and all it symbolises about masculinity). While Thelma may have learned a particularly polite way of robbing people from J.D. ('I've always believed

Louise hearing about Thelma's most recent crime

if done right, armed robbery doesn't have to be a totally unpleasant experience'), she improves upon his routine, making it her own.

This rescripting of the role of the outlaw with a feminine twist allows for many scenes of crime to be highly comedic rather than threatening. This element of wacky humour has led several critics to define *Thelma & Louise* as borrowing on the genre of the screwball comedy, with its snappy dialogue and clever female heroines.[40] Screwball comedy, a genre very popular in the 30s, is usually based on the clever, sexual banter of a couple who don't know that they are supposed to be together, but who eventually find their way to each other through a set of foibles, mistaken identities and other plot ploys. One of the most beloved of screwball road comedies is Frank Capra's 1934 classic *It Happened One Night*, with Clark Gable as a reporter and Claudette Colbert as a runaway heiress, in which she expertly stops a car by hitching her skirt above her knee and he teaches her how to dunk a doughnut in coffee.

In no scene in *Thelma & Louise* is screwball humour more apparent than when the two women are pulled over by a policeman while speeding through the desert. Though this scene follows a number of scenes in which the film has become darker and contemplative – as when Louise stands out in the canyon thinking and then refuses to talk to Thelma about Texas – the film mediates consistently between moments of serious self-reflection and the exhilaration and giddiness of things out of control. When the police car's lights begin flashing behind them, the women go into screwball panic mode, with Thelma reverting to her previous childlike behaviour ('Oh God, please don't let us get caught, God, please, please, please'). As the policeman pulls them over, his motor racing and bullhorn blaring 'Turn off your engine', Louise watches him in the rearview mirror, exclaiming, 'Oh my God, it's a Nazi.' Here, intimidating them with his posture and dark sunglasses, he refers back to the policeman in *Psycho*, who Marion sees framed in the window when she wakes up on the side of the road, his large sunglasses defining his face. The really comic twist of the scene comes, however, when Louise asks, 'Am I in trouble, officer?' and he replies, 'As far as I'm concerned,

yes ma'am, you're in a lot of trouble,' the way a parent would speak to a child. At this point it is clear that he doesn't know who they are; in fact, he is treating them like he would treat another speeder, as someone he has authority over, who is, in a child's terms, in 'big trouble'. We realise that the joke is on him and, at that moment, Thelma pulls her gun on him.

Just as when Thelma robs the store, the humour of this scene hinges on Louise's (and, by extension, the audience's) surprise at Thelma's new-found confidence as an outlaw. When Thelma tells Louise to take the policeman's gun and shoot the radio, the comedy comes from the fact that only Thelma knows the purpose of this and so becomes exasperated when Louise shoots the AM/FM radio instead ('The police radio, Louise, Jesus Christ!'). As the policeman, formerly so authoritative, begins to weep and flinch with every fired shot, the audience shares Louise's and his fear about what Thelma will do. She imitates the policeman's manner of speech, ordering him to 'step to the back of the car' in the same way that he had ordered Louise. She is transformed, her confidence firm. When she shoots air holes into the trunk of the car, the shots take place off camera. Has she shot him, we wonder. It is really not until he begins to plead to her about his wife and kids, and she retorts, in screwball fashion, 'You be sweet to 'em. Especially your wife. My husband wasn't sweet to me, look how I turned out,' that this tension turns to relief.

Confronted by the police officer

Just as Thelma and Louise are polite outlaws, always apologising for their actions and attempting to explain them, Thelma's relentless perkiness, which transforms into a more complex optimism, is central to providing the film's screwball tone. When told by Louise that the police have decided to charge them with murder and that they have to decide if they want to come in dead or alive, Thelma replies, 'Gosh, didn't he say anything positive at all?' In a certain sense, this level of comedy becomes increasingly important as the women get further away and hence closer to being caught. At one point Thelma begins to laugh convulsively, as she imagines Harlan's surprise that they were not what he thought ('He sure wasn't expecting that! Suck my dick … boom!'). Louise is not amused, but as Thelma is telling it, with a kind of adolescent laughter that takes hold of her and reduces her to tears, it does sound funny. Yet, she also moves in a moment from laughing to calm seriousness, catching her

'The police radio, Louise, Jesus Christ!'
'My husband wasn't sweet to me, look how I turned out'

breath. In this slippage between comedy and tragedy, seriousness and irreverence, this scene acts as a microcosm for the film overall. This mix of contradictory tones is reflected later when, as the police are closing in and their options are running out, Louise asks Thelma, 'How do you like the vacation so far?'

There is a certain sense in which Thelma's transformation, prompted by Louise's collapse and schooled by J.D.'s demonstration of how to commit robbery, can also be seen to be ultimately tied to her relationship to the gun. What is a gun but, of course, the ultimate signifier of both masculinity and law? The role of the gun as a symbol of masculine power and authority has long been a staple of the movies, from the western to the outlaw film. Its relationship to male sexuality, now laughably obvious in its role as the ultimate phallic symbol, is underscored in such films as *Bonnie and Clyde*. Both Louise and Thelma begin the film with a dislike of guns. When Thelma puts her gun in her purse – a gun that we learn later she has refused to use or to learn to shoot – she holds it as if it were a piece of dirty laundry, while Louise shrieks with surprise when she sees it. Yet the first time that Louise uses the gun she does so with familiarity.

Its presence in her possession changes everything about the women's fate. It is clear that Harlan would have raped Thelma if Louise had not had a gun, since it was the only thing that stopped him. The gun is the device that allows Louise to speak in the rape scene, to reinterpret his behaviour, and to finally speak the action of shooting him for his sexist threats. Indeed, the gun allows the women to take possession of their bodies, to refuse to let men and, by extension, patriarchal society dictate their meaning. The possession of a gun allows Thelma to get them money and gives her a new-found confidence. It allows them to teach the truck driver a lesson, to put the all-knowing policeman in his place and to keep going towards the border. Indeed, it is her ease with holding a gun and fearlessness in using it that leads Thelma to finally conclude, 'I just feel like I've got a knack for this shit.'

It could be argued that it is specifically because the film presents guns as empowering objects that it promoted controversy. While the

violence of Louise's killing of Harlan is clearly established as an act with consequences, it is not necessarily presented as a regrettable act in the film. Indeed, it is one of the two scenes, along with blowing up the truck, that were most likely to prompt yells of approval when *Thelma & Louise* was screened in theatres. So, while we are meant to understand that Thelma's and Louise's lives are transformed by the gun, and that their use of it changes everything in their lives, that transformation is presented in the film as a positive one. They become aware, have new experiences and become much happier. They come to an understanding, one could even say at an existential level, about the meaning of life. At one point, Thelma says, 'I feel awake, wide awake. I don't remember ever feelin' this awake. Everything looks different.' There is no getting around the fact that the gun is the instrument that facilitates these changes, for without it, they would have been victims rather than agents of their fate.

But what does it mean for this film to show us the empowerment of a gun? It means at one level that the film is enacting the ways in which we live in a society that awards to weapons physical and transformative power. The gun has played a central role in American mythology as an instrument of self-actualisation. Yet the film is also addressing the question of what happens when women get guns and use them, not only to defend themselves but to also use them in anger, as men can do. It is

'I feel awake'

traditional, of course, for the pleasure of watching the outlaw to be tempered by our understanding that within the framework of Hollywood film they must be punished in some way. It is inarguable that Thelma and Louise cannot return in any way to the society whose laws they have broken without consequences, but the film is ambiguous about the degree to which they are punished or their agency taken away. Even Callie Khouri and Susan Sarandon have argued in interviews that the women had to pay a price for their actions, or, as Khouri puts it, 'they were never intended as role models, for God's sake. I don't want anybody doing anything they saw in this movie.'[41] Yet, it is central to the film's message that these women are liberated, have fun and are empowered through their experience of using a gun. While this is a fairly common narrative of liberation, it was clearly deeply disruptive for this story to be told for women.

One of the common misinterpretations of *Thelma & Louise* is that it is a female revenge film, one in which two women take out their anger against men on a group of hapless strangers. This is a convenient category, given that female revenge films are a genre not very friendly to female characters in which the potential of women for violence is contained within plot scenarios that either demonise them or destroy them in some way. *Fatal Attraction* (1987), *Body Heat* (1981) and *Black Widow* (1987) are films in which femmes fatales wreak havoc on the lives of innocent men. Yet, a close examination of the motivations that guide *Thelma & Louise* makes this comparison ineffectual. This is not a film about revenge so much as it is a story of bad luck, impulsive action and the consequences of violence. Susan Sarandon has argued strenuously on this point:

The thing that separates this from a revenge movie with two males, for instance, is that there is a moral price to be paid by me for losing it, as you learn later, because I had been raped. I go into some kind of little trance there and just overreact. But I think the whole rest of the movie from that point on operates under the knowledge for this character that she is going to have to pay a price, and that there is no joy, really, in that revenge. It was important for me, as the movie went on, to try and figure out why these things keep happening, not to make it about getting even. So we tried in all the rest of the scenes to ask questions, or to make it clear, that she's on some kind of search for an understanding of this moment. When I take off all my jewelry and my watch, I think I'm preparing to go into a zone where she feels she had to pay some kind of a price. That was very much in my mind from that moment on in the film.[42]

The central role played by the gun in prompting the women to act in ways they would not have otherwise points away from revenge as a motive. *Thelma & Louise* has often been criticised for being unrealistic in having a woman like Thelma becoming sexually involved with a hitchhiker not long after another stranger had tried to rape her. Yet, it is central to the story that the women are not seeking revenge for the past acts of men against them, rather that they are on a journey of liberation. These are women who have spent their lives trying to negotiate men's needs and are now discovering the thrill of letting that burden go. They have lived lives of accommodation, as exemplified by Thelma's description of Darryl. 'He is an asshole, most of the time I just let it slide,' and Louise's motto, 'You get what you settle for.' For Thelma, her liberation by Louise from what Harlan was trying to do was a much more profound experience than her near rape.

The extent to which the film is realistic about the experience of rape or attempted rape has been central to debates about it among feminist film critics. Does Thelma behave like a rape victim? Does Louise? Many critics have charged that Thelma, while she may look roughed up in the initial scene, recovers too quickly from her experience. She bears no bruises, has no visible wounds and seems to move on, flirting with J.D. a day later. As one critic writes,

Directly after the assault her knees are covered with bruises but she exhibits no other physical or emotional reaction. Instead her character continues to evolve along the lines of fake movie logic. From rape, to murder, to saying 'Fuck you' to her husband, to an affair with a hitchhiker, all in twenty-four hours. In real life, of course, very few battered and assaulted women would

leap into a light-hearted, passionate, and sexually awakening one-night stand with a man they did not know. This is designed to make the film more palatable.[43]

But is Thelma a victim of rape? Isn't it precisely because Louise saves her with the gun that she can move forward? Later in the film she says,

That guy was hurtin' me. And if you hadn't come out when you did, he woulda hurt me a lot worse. And probably nothin' woulda happened to him. Cause everybody did see me dancin' with him all night. They woulda made out like I asked for it. My life would have been ruined a whole lot worse than it is now. At least now I'm havin' some fun. And I'm not sorry that son of a bitch is dead. I'm just sorry that it was you that did it and not me.

Thelma articulates her experience as one of having escaped rape. In other words, the empowerment of the rape scene is precisely the way in which the women take control of their bodies and resist Harlan's assault. Thelma's transformation after this scene demonstrates her sense of power at dictating her own body. Access to freedom is erotic.

At the same time, it is also possible to see the long-term effects of sexual assault on Louise. Although her experience in Texas is never specified in the film, all indications are that she was raped. She is

Thelma, the morning after

well versed in rape law, which prompts more than anything else her motive to run after shooting Harlan. If we accept the way that Sarandon saw the character, her shooting of Harlan takes place in a kind of post-traumatic trance, in which his lack of remorse triggers her long underlying anger.

Yet the film's most important statement on the question of the law and rape is precisely in its premise, from the moment that the shooting takes place, that the women have no choice but to evade the law. Their crime is their inability to stay within the law; as Dargis puts it, their 'crime isn't murder, it's subjectivity'.[44] They become outlaws, that is, outside the law, because of both the nuance of self-defence law and the reality of rape law. Louise knows that she did not shoot Harlan in self-defence. They were, in fact, walking away. In Thelma's childlike world, they should go to the police and tell the truth, that Harlan tried to rape her. But Louise also knows that the fact that Thelma was flirting and dancing with Harlan would be used in court to show that Thelma was a willing partner to Harlan's sexual advances: 'Just about a hundred goddamn people saw you dancing cheek to cheek with him all night. Whose gonna believe that?! We just don't live in that kind of a world, Thelma.'

What is that kind of world that Louise is describing? What would it mean for their actions against Harlan to be justifiable by law? What would a world possibly be in which they could turn themselves in after the shooting and receive fair treatment? In other words, what would it mean for the system to actually work for them at that moment? Louise shoots Harlan because he triggers her memory of assault, but also because it is clear that he has learned nothing from being threatened by the gun, that he would in that moment rape Thelma or any other woman if he could. Yet, there is no law to justify Louise's act.

It is in this moment that the film takes a particular position on the question of women and the law, establishing that there are fundamental ways in which the law does *not* protect women and that the law is, in essence, unfair to their experience. As Thelma says, 'The law is some tricky shit.' *Thelma & Louise* presents Louise's act of murder as not legally justifiable, but morally justifiable, and in that ambiguity, it questions women's relationship to the law. Time and time again in the script the women characters say that they are not sorry that Harlan is dead; they regret breaking the law and the consequences of that, but they do not regret the act itself.

It is a fundamental aspect of rape trials that rape victims describe the legal process as a kind of second violation. Their sexual histories and their clothing styles are investigated, and any element of their behaviour that could be construed as 'asking for it' is dredged up. Men accused of rape use as one of their primary defences that the women led them on, were willing partners, and that the sex was consensual. And who wouldn't, in that context? The misunderstandings between men and women over their intentions and actions are particular acute on issues of sexuality and intent. Louise knows the minute she tells Thelma to get the car that their case would never hold up, that Thelma has broken that rule because she wanted to 'have fun'. Yet, she is also clear that what happened was not Thelma's fault, as she says near the end of their journey: 'Damn it Thelma, if there is one thing you should know by now, this wasn't your fault!'

It is one of the strengths of the film that while we know that something terrible happened to Louise in Texas, most likely that she was raped, the details are withheld. Louise refuses to discuss it with Thelma and Hal never states exactly what it is that he has found out. There are many ways to imagine how this scene could have been played out, with Louise's memories being acted out in flashback or her finally telling Thelma what happened, but her silence carries far more power. Not only does it allow the film's message about women who have been the victim of violence from men to remain a general one, rather than equated with a particular crime, but it also reveals the depth of Louise's experience. That is a place where she does not want to go because it is too painful.

This explains why Louise refuses to drive through Texas. On the surface, this would appear to be an irrational decision, after all, as Thelma puts it, they are running for their lives ('Can't you make an exception?'). Louise's decision, however, indicates more than her refusal to re-enter the state where something terrible happened to her. She is not only staying away from memories, she is staying away from a particular style of law enforcement. As she says, 'You shoot off a guy's head with his pants down, believe me, Texas is not the place you wanna get caught!' Texas, it would appear, is an extreme version of the law that they are running away from, though it is also, we learn later, where Louise learned to shoot so well. In national mythology, Texas is inevitably the most American (that is, pronounced 'Amurican') of states, with its cowboys, cattle ranches, big sky, barbecues and rodeos. It is also one of the most conservative states in terms of law enforcement and has the toughest laws in the country. Texas is known, for instance, for executing the largest number of death-row inmates and granting them the fewest rights to appeal. The image of Texas combines that of the brutal aspects of the law with the mystique of the outlaw.

In *Thelma & Louise*, Texas is not only the place where you wouldn't want to get caught after killing a guy with his pants down, it is the primary signifier of patriarchy, masculinity and the law.[45] The ambiguity of the moral stance of the film – in which Harlan's death is legally wrong but never regretted – means that the two women are on the run from the kind of law in which there is no recourse but punishment. Texas represents the law of the father, the law of the nation and the laws of men that Thelma and Louise have broken. In this sense, Louise is only operating under the illusion that they can drive around Texas, because Texas is everywhere. It stands for what they cannot escape, the reason why they can't go back; it's the symbol of American masculinity at its extremes of brutality and morality.

For these reasons, Texas offers a clue to why the women end up where they do. They cannot return to Arkansas, not only because they have killed a man there but because they have tasted what it means to be liberated from the routines of their dreary lives. Once they have experienced the thrill of the new horizon and a sense of power, they cannot go back to lives of reduced expectations. When Thelma says to Louise, 'Something's crossed over in me and I can't go back,' she is

referring not to the legal circumstances that prevent her from returning to her former life, but the psychic changes that would make it impossible for her to put up with what she tolerated before. But is it really possible within the framework of the film to imagine a positive scenario by which the women could end up 'drinkin' margaritas by the sea'? If they are on the run from patriarchal law is there any place where they could end up that would be considered outside of it? It would have been very problematic for the film to end with the women making it to Mexico, not only because of the false promise it would provide but because Mexico is not outside of what they are fleeing. It would also have been very difficult to have ended the film with the two women being arrested and going to prison, since that ending would have undercut not only its humour but also its message of liberation. Indeed, it seems to have been inevitable that the film end with the two women continuing on in a mystical sense, an ending that is both tragic and idealistic at the same time.

There is a scene in the script, which Khouri has stated she regrets is not in the final film, in which the two women talk about what their greatest fears were before they took their trip. Louise's worst fear was to end up in 'some crummy apartment with one of those little dogs' and Thelma's worst fear was about getting old with Darryl: 'It's bad enough I have to get old, but doin' it with Darryl around is only gonna make it

'Something's crossed over in me and I can't go back'

worse. I mean, I don't think he's gonna be very nice about it.' In this sense, both are running away from lives that are about stasis, lives of confinement with no sense of possibilities. This defines, of course, a very unironic embrace of the ideals of the road movie.

As the women's journey nears completion, their role as outlaws is increasingly eclipsed by their definition as criminals. As they drive toward the Grand Canyon, law enforcement technology begins to define them more and more. Descriptions of them repeat over the police radios as the helicopter hones in on them, representing a particular kind of knowing – that of the suspect/criminal:

Suspect driving: Louise Elizabeth Sawyer, white female, d.o.b. 10-17-55, red hair, brown eyes, five foot seven inches tall, 120 pounds. Suspect: Thelma Yvonne Dickinson, white female, d.o.b. 11-27-56, red hair, green eyes, five foot ten inches tall, 130 pounds. Both subjects armed and extremely dangerous. Approach with caution. [Wanted in] New Mexico and Arizona on felony warrants for armed robbery, kidnaping a law enforcement officer, assault with a deadly weapon ...

In these descriptions, reduced to their police files, the women are transformed from the subject positions of outlaws to that of criminals. It is only in continuing to drive forward that the women can prevent these descriptions from defining who they are.

Pursued in their final run

The ending of *Thelma & Louise*, in which the two women decide to keep driving away from the law, is one of the film's most controversial aspects. It is important that when Callie Khouri began writing her script, she started not only with the idea 'two women go on a crime spree' but also with the image of a car flying into the Grand Canyon. The story was conceived from the beginning as one in which the women are on a journey that cannot end back in society. Yet Khouri is adamant that the film does not end with suicide:

It always struck me as preposterous that people saw it as a suicide. I don't even think of them as dead. I just wasn't in any way prepared for people to say, 'God, they killed themselves? What kind of message is that?' I want to say, 'It's the message you came up with, not me.' To me, the ending was symbolic, not literal. I mean, come on, read a book. We did everything possible to make sure you didn't see a literal death. That you didn't see the car land, you didn't see a big puff of smoke come up out of the canyon. You were left with the image of them flying. They flew away, out of this world and into the mass unconscious. Women who are completely free from all the shackles that restrain them have no place in this world. The world is not big enough to support them. They will be brought down if they stay here. They weren't going to be brought down. So let them go. I loved that ending and I loved the imagery. After all they went through I didn't want anybody to be able to touch them.

The car's flight

The decision that the women make is not to die, but to keep going. As Thelma says, 'Let's keep going, go.' In the end, the women leave the world of law behind. While this ending has often been compared to that of *Butch Cassidy and the Sundance Kid*, which also ends in a freeze frame, there are crucial differences in tone in the two endings. Butch Cassidy and Sundance, having been stripped of all their possessions and run out of escape routes, decide to go out shooting. Thelma and Louise do not turn to shoot, even though Louise contemplates it. Instead they decide, when faced with a veritable army of state troopers, to continue going on the only route left to them, over the cliff.

The film's construction of this final journey of the women out over the canyon has been underscored by its soundtrack, an ensemble of songs, both rock and country, that speak in relatively subtle ways about liberation and flying away. Martha Reeves sings about a 'wild night' in which 'the wind will catch your feet and send you flying', and in a playful tune, B.B. King sings about giving advice to many folks, including 'the Queen of England':

Better not look down, if you want to keep on flyin'
Put the hammer down, keep it full speed ahead
Better not look back or you might just end up cryin'
You can keep it movin' if you don't look down ...

'Go'

Ridley Scott shot two endings for the film. The first, which is in the final film, shows the two women making their decision with tears in their eyes. They kiss and then drive forward toward the cliff. Intercut with scenes of Hal running after them, the car approaches the edge and they clasp hands as Louise puts her foot on the gas. We see the car fly out over the cliff, a hub cap falling from it and, as it flies forward, the image freezes the car in midair and fades to white. It then almost immediately goes into a credit sequence that recaps many scenes in the film, which has the effect of both provoking sadness that these vital women are gone and of making them feel still alive.

In the alternative ending to the film, the car continues to fly out over the canyon then begins to turn and descend within it until it is cut off from view. Hal runs to the edge of the cliff and looks down as the helicopter flies past him. The state troopers put down their rifles and walk toward the cliff. There is a long shot of Hal, looking down, his face pained. In the final shot, we see a car driving down the road that opened the film, leaving a cloud of dust. While this alternative ending is more explicit in its message that the two women continue on, with the implication in the final shot that they continue to drive forward, it is also a much darker way to end the film. The image of the car continuing to fall into the canyon is harrowing, implying much more specifically that it fell to the canyon floor. Further, this ending gives much more focus to

The alternative ending

the reaction of the men who watch the women drive off the cliff. Its overall tone is one of shock and regret, and it implies that they, and in particular Hal, feel sorrow for what has happened. While this is tempered by the implication that the women, at least figuratively, get away and keep driving, it shifts the emphasis from them to the men they leave behind. As Scott says, this version 'eclipsed what their decision was' and he wanted the ending to be focused on the women instead: 'I wanted it to be a happy ending. … It's noble … a touch of class.'

Hal is a liminal figure here, caught between the women and the law. He has transgressed the space of gender relations by being too sympathetic to the women and hence has lost the confidence of the FBI. When he yells at Max, 'How long are these women going to be fucked over?', he is coded as an hysterical man rather than a law enforcement official. He runs towards the women because he knows that the troopers will not shoot him in the back – he still believes that he can save them. Yet, here, of course, Hal is wrong. The moment that Thelma and Louise decide to drive forward, they are no longer subjects within the law of the land, and they do not want to be saved or jailed by this well-intentioned man.

What does it mean that the two women kiss before they drive off the cliff? The ending of the film asserts the primacy of their friendship in their lives, as they make their momentous decision together and clasp hands as they fly out over the cliff. This bond has been alternatively

Hal tries once again to save them

interpreted as a lesbian bond and as that of heterosexual friendship. This first interpretation can be situated in the context of closeted representation. For many years, the inability of mainstream Hollywood film to represent alternative sexualities has produced a set of signals that are understood in code. In the codes of closeted lesbianism representation, a kiss between women on the screen, no matter how innocently it is presented on the surface, is a sign of lesbian desire. Many viewers of *Thelma & Louise* have felt that the film allows for this interpretation: that the reason the two women can't go back to the world of patriarchal society is not only because of the law but because of their desire for each other. It may be precisely because the kiss between the two women occurs at the end of the film, just before they take off and 'leave' this world, that the film can be seen as presenting them as desiring each other, since the story is then left to the viewer.[46] After all, they have been constructed in many ways as a couple, in particular in the film's playing off the conventions of the screwball genre, which always ends with the couple married. They have left their men and the world of men behind, hence their embrace solidifies their relationship, as all final screen kisses do.

However, while many fans and some theorists have understood *Thelma & Louise* as offering an image of women's love and desire for each other, the most common interpretation of this final kiss is that it symbolises a union of two heterosexual women as friends – or a 'mystical' marriage that is not about sexuality but, in the tradition of the buddy film, the power of friendship. Indeed, for many, including the women who worked on the film, the strength of the film is in its representation of the complex bonds of friendship that are formed between heterosexual women, a relationship that is usually represented in Hollywood films negatively as competitive and jealous. Yet, it is important to note that the film itself actually accommodates both of these viewing positions, leaving open the meaning of the women's embrace. This ambiguity was central to much of its success with women viewers. In this sense, *Thelma & Louise* raises important questions about the nature of identification.

Identification and the Gaze

The question of who we identify with when we are watching films and how we feel connections to the characters on the screen has been central to film theory. Given that viewers are encouraged by the apparatus of cinema – with its dark room, big screen and spectacle – to sublimate their sense of self in order to identify with and/or fantasise about the actions on the screen, considerable attention has been paid by film scholars to the nuances of the act of spectatorship. The issue of difference has become crucial to understanding the process of viewership, as theories of gender, race and other cultural differences have questioned any concept of a general viewer of the screen. For the most part, issues of cinematic identification have remained within the realm of academic publishing. Yet, in the debate over *Thelma & Louise*, the issue of the gaze and viewer identification became a part of public discourse. Much of the anxiety surrounding the film focused on who viewers would identify with in the absence of likable male protagonists and what potential effects that might have on viewers.

In 70s and 80s feminist film theory, analyses of the spectator concentrated on the issue of the gaze. Cinema is a medium about looking – specifically the pleasures of looking at others – and the power dynamics of looking and being looked at. A particular area of feminist film theory in the 70s, which was sparked by a now-famous article by Laura Mulvey entitled 'Visual Pleasure and Narrative Cinema', used theories of psychoanalysis to analyse how in traditional Hollywood cinema, women become the 'object of the male gaze'.[47] It was Mulvey's theory that the role of women in cinema is to be on display for the gaze of the protagonist, the viewing audience and the camera, all of which are presumed to be male. Mulvey's theory was criticised for its pessimistic view that Hollywood cinema allowed no agency to the female spectator, and it has been rethought and reworked as a theory ever since by many theorists, including Mulvey herself. Many current views on the gaze focus on the multiplicity of gazes and identifications that might exist in a viewing context, for instance the ways in which viewers might identify with particular aspects of a character, or across gender, or against the intended meaning of a film. In the complexity of contemporary image culture, men are increasingly imaged as the object of a gaze and women are sometimes seen as those who can look with power.

In *Thelma & Louise*, there is an engagement with many different kinds of gazes. The two women, who are, we should not forget, both beautiful Hollywood stars, are the object of the male gaze, sometimes in very obvious ways. When they arrive at the Silver Bullet saloon, for instance, the men turn and watch them as they walk across the room. Various men, from Harlan to the truck driver, make clear to them that they are seen as sexual objects and as potentially possessable through the gaze. They are called 'kewpie dolls' (by Harlan), 'peaches' (by Jimmy) and 'beavers' (by the trucker), as well as 'girls' (by Hal and others). However, the film departs from any conventional representation of the gendered gaze by playing with the whole question of what it means when we look. Thelma and Louise gaze back, they look with agency, if not desire, and they question many of the gazes upon them. As Louise is walking through a gas station at one point, she looks back at one of the men staring at her and challenges him with 'What are you lookin' at?'

The question of looking, and who is looking at who, is actually a constant theme in the film. The women are on the road, where one of the primary activities, of course, is that of looking. They are driving a convertible, a vehicle in which a primary function is to be looked at.

The belligerent truck driver

Indeed, the issue of their conspicuousness in the car is a constant tension in the plot – so much of their pleasure on the road, and the pleasure of the viewers in watching them, is tied up in the convertible. In addition, many of the film's scenes of self-reflection take place before mirrors. Both women go through physical transformations in the film, with Thelma getting rid of her frilly clothes and girlish make-up, and Louise losing her tight hairdo and throwing away her lipstick, and much of this process of shedding certain codes of femininity takes place in front of mirrors. The mirror has long been a symbol of female narcissism, if not an essential tool to the construction of femininity. When Louise goes to the 'little girls'

room' at the bar, she has to fight her way to a small patch of the mirror as the women crane and shove their way to their reflections. After the shooting, Louise looks in the mirror only to see to her horror that there is a small speck of blood on her cheek, which she anxiously attempts to wipe away. Later, when she throws away her lipstick, she turns away from the mirror as if in despair at its reflection. For Louise, the mirror becomes, through the course of the film, something to turn away from, to avoid, as if it were a kind of looking back.

For Thelma, however, the mirror is a tool of empowerment, a way of experimenting with new ways of looking. Thelma uses the car mirror to try out new styles, like pretending to smoke, and to look at the world around her surreptitiously. One of the things that she sees in that mirror is the

Louise wipes away the speck of blood

hitchhiker J.D. While she is waiting in the car for Louise and putting on her lipstick in the mirror, she adjusts it to watch him walking by with his duffle bag. Her gaze, we learn later, is directed in particular at his butt, which she assesses in relation to Darryl's. The film establishes that one of Thelma's pleasures is watching J.D. ('I love to watch him go').

This is all played for humour in the film, but clearly there is more than a comedic reversal at work here. Thelma, who began the film as a classic feminine character, unable to get out from under the control of her philandering husband, has found a way to talk about desire through looking. Importantly, the film affirms her desire by making J.D. the object of the camera's gaze. Indeed, in the sex scene with Thelma and J.D., the camera spends much more time focused on his body than hers,

J.D. observed

moving in a slow shot down his naked torso (the DVD programme notes actually call this scene 'J.D.'s Nice Abs'). This is all underscored by Brad Pitt's star quality (this was his breakthrough role, before he became a mega-star) and his character's role as a charming, seductive, yet unreliable man. It is not incidental, for instance, that his character's name could be short for James Dean.

What does it mean that the film not only establishes Thelma's gaze upon J.D. as one of agency, but also privileges it as well? For many of the film's critics, this was just another example of the script wanting to have it both ways – to let women leer after men while they punished men for looking at them. Yet it could hardly be argued that J.D. is disempowered by the gaze of the women and the camera upon him as a sexual being. Rather, the film shows the complexity of the power dynamics of these gazes. J.D. is sexualised by the gaze upon him and he uses that sexuality to get what he wants – pleasure and money. Thelma and Louise reject the unwanted gazes of strange men upon them, yet take pleasure in other looks. They take the power away from certain gazes upon them by staring back or pointing a gun. They are subject to the gazes of the law – the gaze of the surveillance camera, the gaze upon them in the final scene from the approaching helicopter, the gaze of their distant figures through the scopes of the trooper's rifles – which they evade by driving away, out of sight. All of these scenes demonstrate the extent to which

J.D. in the camera's gaze

the film defies traditional formulas of the gaze, and shows the complexity of the power relations of looking. Indeed, the film begins with the two women taking a Polaroid photograph of themselves. This image, which is often used to illustrate the film, shows the two women smiling together before a camera that they hold themselves. Here, they control the camera, even as they are, by implication, still framed within the codes of the male gaze. This photograph appears again in the final shots of the film, when it flies out of the backseat of the car as Louise steps on the gas and the car flies over the canyon's edge. It is now an image of their former selves, no longer relevant.

In the rifle's gaze
Photographs and memories

One of the primary aspects of theories of the gaze is the question of who viewers identify with on the cinematic screen. It was originally understood by theorists like Laura Mulvey that spectators identify with characters of the same gender, hence the tradition of male protagonists means that only male audience members could identify with the central protagonists who further the narrative. Crude versions of Mulvey's argument stated that this meant that female spectators had only the option of masochism (to identify with the women on the screen who were only the objects of the gaze or were punished in it in some way) or transvestism (to identify across gender, as men). However arcane this theory may appear now, it is worth noting that one of the primary aspects of the debate about *Thelma & Louise* was how it would accommodate male viewers for whom there was no 'proper' male to identify with. Unlike a traditional 'women's picture', for which such a question might not arise, this was a road movie with car chases and guns and action, and, by implication, a movie men should be able to identify with.

Geena Davis was quoted at the time as stating, 'If you're feeling threatened, you're identifying with the wrong character.'[48] Khouri said, 'Most guys don't relate to the truck driver or the rapist, and if they do, their problems are bigger than this movie.'[49] Both women were thus articulating a central aspect of film identification – that this film demands of spectators that they identify with the women in the film, whether they themselves are male or female. And why not? Haven't we all wanted to break out, hit the road and feel a sense of liberation? Does this mean, as many critics charged, that the film was advocating that film-goers imitate the women on film? Of course not, indeed, no film does. But what was missing from the debate, yet which is so clear from Davis's comment, is that identification with characters in a film is never a simple process of fantasising about being them so much as it is about identifying with particular traits, emotions and actions. If women have spent the history of cinema identifying with aspects of male characters, why can't male spectators identify with female protagonists? While it seems that many male audience members did just that, it is also clear that the controversy surrounding this film was deeply rooted in its demand for cross-gender identification.

Perhaps it makes sense to consider the ways in which the film is felt to be transformative by some of its fans. As a story with an ambiguous ending, one in which the women appear to be both participating in a joint suicide and simultaneously escaping the world that wants to hem them in, *Thelma & Louise* sparked many fantasies about what could have happened to the women. Indeed, one of these was humorously spun out by Sarandon and Davis themselves when they presented an award for editing at the Oscar ceremonies the following year:

Davis: In our film, *Thelma & Louise*, the way the final scene was edited, it was sort of left ambiguous what really happened to us at the end.
Sarandon: Ambiguous, Geena? Our T-bird went off the edge of the Grand Canyon. That's not ambiguous.
Davis: Well, nobody saw us land, did they?
Sarandon: What did you think people thought happened?
Davis: We could have grabbed onto something or we were going fast, maybe we made it to the other side. Susan, if we didn't survive the crash, there's no sequel.
Sarandon: We could have bounced!
Davis: There you go.

While humorously pointing to a central aspect of the script, that is, whether we are to read it literally, as many viewers did, or figuratively, as Khouri and Scott intended, this dialogue also reminds us that in the world of Hollywood cinema, characters are resurrected from the dead all the time, that it is precisely the carefully constructed artifice and abstraction of the cinema that allows us to suspend belief and allow for the unlikely sequel. In other words, it's just a movie.

Even so, the film has often been treated as a life-altering experience by many of its fans. It would be easy to be cynical about such an effect, but it is important to take note of the shock of recognition that representations can sometimes provide. Sarandon has said that two films during her career – *The Rocky Horror Picture Show*, a 1975 film with an enormous cult following (people often dress up and perform along with the film), and *Thelma & Louise* – produced huge amounts of fan mail about how people felt empowered by them: 'Strangely enough, I got letters when *Thelma & Louise* came out from people who said to me, "I live in such-and-such and the first time you saved my life was with *The Rocky Horror Show*, and now I've seen *Thelma & Louise* and I'm leaving." And so they had the same reaction to both movies at different times of their lives.'

Evidence of the film's capacity to empower can also be seen in the way in which it is appropriated by a number of website groups in which women define themselves as members of Thelma & Louise, 'a group of classy, gutsy ladies'. It may be that many of these scenarios reduce the film to a neat set of sequences, with its nuances gone, yet they are also about understanding the narrative of the film as one of liberation. It is a strength of the film that it accommodates a range of interpretations, so that it can be understood both as comedy and tragedy, lesbian and straight, as triumphant and sobering. Importantly, it ends by affirming not only the journey of liberation but the bonds of friendship. Here, instead of B.B. King singing about never looking down, as in the original script, the film ends with a song by Glenn Frey that can either be understood as a love song or a song about the power of friendship to change our lives:

Til we find a bridge across forever
Til this grand illusion brings us home
You and I will always be together
From this day on you'll never walk alone
You're a part of me, I'm a part of you
Wherever we may travel, whatever we go through
Whatever time they take away
It cannot change the way we feel today
So hold me close and soon you'll feel it too
You're part of me and I am part of you.

Finally, we end with two women sitting in a car and making a decision. They have tasted power. They cannot go back, only forward. Their final gaze, before they drive off the cliff and into the imaginary, is at each other. Clasping hands, they decide to continue onward. They make a choice. That is all we need to know.

Notes

1 Richard Schickel, 'Gender Bender', *Time*, 24 June 1991, pp. 52–6.

2 Cynthia Heimel, 'Tongue in Chic', *Village Voice*, 9 July 1991, p. 37.

3 John Leo, 'Toxic Feminism on the Big Screen', *U.S. News & World Report*, 10 June 1991, p. 20. Leo states in his essay that he was prompted to write his column after a friend, 'no faintheart but a strong and extremely successful woman in the movie business', told him that it was very disturbing. According to Manohla Dargis, this was reportedly screenwriter and director Nora Ephron, who has made such films as *Heartburn*, *When Harry Met Sally* and *You've Got Mail*. See Manohla Dargis, 'Guns N' Poses', *Village Voice*, 16 July 1999, p. 22.

4 Richard Johnson, *Daily News*, quoted in Richard Schickel, 'Gender Bender', p. 52.

5 Quoted in Sheila Johnston, 'Hidden Gender', *The Independent*, 29 June 1991, p. 30.

6 Johnson, *Daily News*.

7 Asa Baber, 'Guerrilla Feminism', *Playboy*, October 1991, p. 45.

8 Leo, 'Toxic Feminism on the Big Screen', p. 20.

9 Baber, 'Guerrilla Feminism', p. 45.

10 Sheila Benson, 'True or False: Thelma & Louise Just Good Ol' Boys?', *Los Angeles Times*, 31 May 1991, p. F1.

11 *Los Angeles Times*, quoted in Johnston, 'Hidden Gender', p. 30.

12 Liz Smith, quoted in Laura Shapiro, 'Women Who Kill Too Much', *Newsweek*, 17 June 1991, p. 63.

13 Janet Maslin, 'Lay Off "Thelma and Louise"', *New York Times*, 16 June 1991, section 2, p. 11.

14 Benson, 'True or False: Thelma & Louise Just Good Ol' Boys?', p. F1.

15 Manohla Dargis, 'The Roads to Freedom', *Sight and Sound*, July 1991, p. 18.

16 Ana Maria Bahiana, 'Callie Khouri', *Cinema Papers* 85, November 1991, p. 36.

17 Lizzie Francke, 'Interview with Callie Khouri', *Guardian*, 9 July 1991, p. 17.

18 Margaret Carlson, 'Is This What Feminism is all About?', *Time*, 24 June 1991, p. 57.

19 Dargis, 'Guns N' Poses', p. 22.

20 Hilton Als, 'Masculine and Feminine', *Village Voice*, 28 May 1991, p. 56.

21 Jodie Burke, 'An Interview with Callie Khouri', in *Thelma & Louise and Something to Talk About: Screenplays*, by Callie Khouri (New York: Grove Press, 1996), pp. ix–x. Unless otherwise noted, all other quotes from Callie Khouri are from this interview.

22 Leo, 'Toxic Feminism on the Big Screen', p. 20.

23 Associated Press, 'Unlikely Suspects are Sought in "Thelma and Louise" Robberies', *New York Times*, 13 August 1995, p. 30.

24 Richard Grenier, 'Killer Bimbos', *Commentary*, September 1991, p. 52.

25 Carl Wayne Arrington, 'Lost in America', *Premiere*, April 1991, p. 108.

26 Jamie Portman, 'Outspoken Actresses Challenge the Big Boys', *Toronto Star*, 25 May 1991, p. H7.

27 Als, 'Masculine and Feminine', p. 56.

28 Shapiro, 'Women Who Kill Too Much', p. 63.

29 Carlson, 'Is This What Feminism is All About?', p. 57.

30 Peter Keough, quoted in Schickel, 'Gender Bender', p. 53.

31 Betsy Sharkey, 'Ridley Scott Tries to Make it Personal', *New York Times*, 18 November 1990, section 2, p. 24.

32 Judith Michaelson, 'Downright Serious',
Los Angeles Times, 12 May 1991, p. 5.
33 Ridley Scott, commentary on DVD of
Thelma & Louise. Unless otherwise noted,
further quotes from Scott are from this
commentary.
34 Amy Taubin, 'Ridley Scott's Road Work',
Sight and Sound, July 1991, p. 18.
35 Arrington, 'Lost in America', p. 108.
36 Taubin, 'Ridley Scott's Road Work',
p. 18.
37 Timothy Corrigan, *A Cinema Without
Walls: Movies and Culture After Vietnam*
(New Brunswick, N.J.: Rutgers University
Press, 1991), pp. 143–5.
38 Steven Cohan and Ina Rae Hark,
'Introduction', *The Road Movie Book*, eds
Steven Cohan and Ina Rae Hark (London:
Routledge, 1997), p. 12.
39 Jay Carr, 'Ms. Maverick', *Press-Telegram*,
25 May 1991, p. C2.
40 Peter Chumo II, 'At the Generic
Crossroads with *Thelma and Louise*', *Post
Script* vol. 13 no. 2, Winter/Spring 1994,
pp. 3–13.
41 Larry Rohter, 'The Third Woman of
"Thelma and Louise"', *New York Times*,
5 June 1991, p. C21.
42 Susan Sarandon, interview with Terry
Gross, 'Fresh Air', National Public Radio,
16 December 1999. All further quotes from
Sarandon are from this interview.
43 Sarah Schulman, 'The Movie
Management of Rape', *Cineaste* vol. 18
no. 4, 1991, p. 34.

44 Dargis, 'Roads to Freedom', p. 17.
45 I am indebted on this point to an
unpublished paper written in 1994 by
Andrew Betterton in my class at the
University of California, San Diego.
46 Cathy Griggers, 'Thelma and Louise and
the Cultural Generation of the New Butch-
Femme', *Film Theory Goes to the Movies*,
eds Jim Collins, Hilary Radner, and Ava
Preacher Collins (London: Routledge,
1993), pp. 129–41.
47 Laura Mulvey, 'Visual Pleasure and
Narrative Cinema', in *Visual and Other
Pleasures* (Bloomington: Indiana University
Press, 1989), pp. 14–26.
48 Rohter, 'The Third Woman of "Thelma
and Louise"', p. C21. Carol Clover notes
that this quote by Davis is evidence that 'a
real corner in gender representation has
been turned in mainstream film history'. She
emphasises that many of these aspects of
identification have been a part of the non-
mainstream tradition of horror films, with
their 'tough-girl heroes'. See Carol Clover,
'Crossing Over', *Film Quarterly*, vol. 45
no. 2, Winter 1991–92, p. 55; and Carol
Clover, *Men, Women, and Chainsaws:
Gender in the Modern Horror Film*
(Princeton, N.J.: Princeton University Press,
1992).
49 Janice C. Shepard, 'Moving into the
Driver's Seat', *Time*, 24 June 1991, p. 55.

Credits

Thelma & Louise

USA
1991

Director
Ridley Scott
Producers
Ridley Scott, Mimi Polk
Screenplay
Callie Khouri
Director of Photography
Adrian Biddle
Editor
Thom Noble
Production Designer
Norris Spencer
Music
Hans Zimmer

©Pathe Entertainment, Inc
Production Companies
Pathe Entertainment
presents
a Percy Main production
a Ridley Scott film
Co-producers
Dean O'Brien, Callie Khouri
Production Accountant
Sam Bernstein
Payroll Supervisor
Patrick Spezialy
**Assistant Production
Accountant**
Stephanie Claxton
Accounting Secretary
Rob Stevens
**Post-production
Accountant**
Arthur Tarry

**Assistant Post-production
Accountant**
Pauline Granby
Production Co-ordinator
Christine Baer
**Assistant Production
Co-ordinator**
Tracy DeFreitas
Unit Production Managers
Dean O'Brien, Mel Dellar
Location Managers
California:
Michael Neale
Utah:
Kenneth Haber
**Assistant Location
Manager**
James M. Kelly
**Post-production
Supervisor**
Garth Thoms
**Post-production
Co-ordinator**
Julie Payne
Assistant to Mr Scott
Cary Burns
Assistant to Ms Polk
Scott Bergstein
Assistant to Ms Sarandon
Phillip Leslie Tomalin Jr
Production Secretary
Diana Campbell-Rice
Location Assistants
Larry Campbell, Patrick
Mignano
Production Assistants
Paul Bellman, Robin Allen,
Kami Turrou
2nd Unit Director
Bobby Bass

First Assistant Directors
Steve Danton
2nd Unit:
J. Tom Archuleta
Second Assistant Director
B. Scott Senechal
**2nd Second Assistant
Director**
Wendolyn Peterson
DGA Trainee
Martin Jedlicka
Script Supervisor
Luca Kouimelis
Casting
Louis DiGiaimo
Casting Associate
Ira Belgrade
Extra Casting
Dan Parada, The Casting
Group
**Aerial Director of
Photography**
David B. Nowell
Aerial Camera Technician
John A. Connell
Camera Operators
Alexander Witt, Michael
Scott
2nd Unit:
Alexander Witt
**First Assistant
Cameramen**
Dan Mindel, Cal Roberts
**Second Assistant
Cameramen**
Stephen Patrick Norman,
Steve Adcock
Clapper Loader
J. Steven Matzinger
Key Grip
Bobby Rose

Best Boy Grip
Audie Aragon
Dolly Grips
Brad Rea, R. Sott Judge
Grips
Erich O. Rose, Kenji Inouye,
Bob Miyamoto, Andy Aguilar,
David Canestro
Chief Lighting Technician
Thomas P. Cox
Best Boy Electrician
Paul Amorelli
Electricians
Joe Rowan, James Cox,
Darrin Pulford, John D.
Smock, Kevin Newett
Generator Operator
Dennis Dodd
Video Assistant
Aaron Katz
Still Photographer
Roland Neveu
**Special Effects
Co-ordinator**
Stan Parks
**Special Effects
Technicians**
Kevin S. Quibell, Todd K.
Jensen, Tim J. Moran, Martin
J. Gibbons, Paul Stewart
Assistant Editors
Chris Peppe, Alexandra
Leviloff, Craig Galloway,
Antonia van Drimmelen
Apprentice Editors
Audrey Evans, David
Richards
Art Director
Lisa Dean
Assistant Art Director
Michael Hirabayashi

Set Designer
Alan Kaye
Set Decorator
Anne Ahrens
Assistant Set Decorator
Ross Harpold
Production Illustrator
Sherman Labby
Greensman
Robert L. Samarzich
Greens Assistant
Lazar Samarzich
Leadman
Kenneth Turek
Swing Gang
Paul A. Hartman, Walter
Berner III, Richard Raymond
Powell, James T. Randol
Property Master
Vic Petrotta Jr
Assistant Property Master
Chuck Roseberry
Property Assistants
Monti Santilli Rainbolt,
Victor F. Petrotta III
**Construction
Co-ordinator**
Richard Bayard
Construction Foremen
Mark Vitale, Roger Janson,
James Olson, Scott Snyder
Paint Foreman
Gary A. Clark
Stand-by Painter
Frank Galvan III
Labour Foremen
Larry R. Wehner,
Addie Flores
Costume Designer
Elizabeth McBride

Key Costumer
Taneia Lednicky
Set Costumers
Janet L. Powell, Nisa Kellner
Make-up Artists
Richard Arrington,
Bonita DeHaven
Hairstylists
Leslie Anne Anderson,
Anthony Cortino,
Karl Wesson
Title Design
Anthony Goldschmidt
Titles/Opticals
Pacific Title
Colour Timer
David Orr
Solo Guitar
Pete Haycock
Music Supervisor
Kathy Nelson
Music Co-ordinator
Blake Lewin
Pathe Music Executive
Joachim H. Hansch
Music Editor
Laura Perlman
Music Recording
Jay Rifkin
Soundtrack
'Little Honey' by John Doe,
David Alvin, performed by
Kelly Willis, produced by
Tony Brown; 'Wild Night' by
Van Morrison, performed by
Martha Reeves, produced
by Richard Perry; 'House of
Hope' by Toni Childs, David
Ricketts, performed by Toni
Childs, produced by David
Ricketts, Toni Childs with

Gavin McKillop; 'I Don't
Want to Love You (But I Do)'
by Paul Kennerly, performed
by Kelly Willis; 'Tennessee
Plates' by John Hiatt, Mike
Porter, performed by Charlie
Sexton, produced by Nile
Rodgers; 'Mercury Blues' by
Robert Geddins, K. C.
Douglas, performed by
Charlie Sexton, produced by
Jeff Lord-Alge, Charlie
Sexton, re-mixed by Don
Smith; 'Badlands'
by/performed by Charlie
Sexton, produced by Nile
Rodgers; 'I Don't Wanna
Play House' by Glenn
Sutton, Billy Sherrill,
performed by Tammy
Wynette; 'Part of Me, Part of
You' by Glenn Frey, Jack
Tempchin, performed by
Glenn Frey, produced by
Don Was, co-produced by
Elliot Scheiner; 'The Way You
Do the Things You Do' by
William Robinson, Robert
Rogers, performed by The
Temptations; 'Kick the
Stones' by/performed by
Chris Whitley, produced by
Malcolm Burn; 'I Can't Untie
You from Me', 'Don't Look
Back' by Holly Knight,
Grayson Hugh, performed
by Grayson Hugh, produced
by Bernard Edwards; 'Drawn
to the Fire' by Pam Tillis,
Stan Webb, performed by
Pam Tillis; 'No Lookin' Back'
by Kenny Loggins, Michael
McDonald, Ed Sanford,
performed by Michael
McDonald; 'The Ballad of
Lucy Jordan' by Shel
Silverstein, performed by
Marianne Faithfull, produced
by Mark Miller Mundy for
Airstream; 'I Can See Clearly
Now' by/performed by
Johnny Nash; 'Better Not
Look Down' by Joe Sample,
Will Jennings, performed by
B.B. King, produced by
Stewart Levine for Oliverea
Productions Ltd

Production Sound Mixer
Keith A. Wester
Boom Operator
Timothy P. Salmon
Re-recording Mixer
Graham Hartstone
**Assistant Re-recording
Mixers**
Nicholas Le Messuier,
Michael Carter
Additional Re-recording
WarnerHollywood Studios,
Jeffrey J. Haboush
Supervising Sound Editor
Jimmy Shields
Assistant Sound Editors
Les Healey, Gordon Davie
Negative Cutter
Bobby Hart
Sound Effects Editor
Bob Risk
ADR Editor
John Poyner
Assistant ADR Editor
Norman Cole

**Transportation
Co-ordinator**
Terry Collis
Transportation Captains
David Trevino, Gerald L.
Sidwell, Lynn Collis
First Aid
Michelle Michael
Projectionist
Lisa Hackler
Craft Service
Tim Gonzales, Gerald
Bowne
Catering
Michelson-Gallo, Gala
Catering
Stunt Co-ordinator
Bobby Bass
Stunt Players
Michael C. Ryan, Kenny
Endoso, Bennie E. Moore Jr,
Buddy Joe Hooker, Billy
Lucas, Greg Barnett, Tony
Epper, David Burton, David
Webster, Steve Boyum,
Hank Hooker, Dick Ziker,
Mary Peters, John Meier,
Ronnie Rondell, Ann Melville,
Norma Howell, Terry Collis,
Bob Dewitt, Bobby Bass
'Louise' Stunt Doubles
Glory Fioramonti,
Marguerite Happy
'Thelma' Stunt Double
Diane Kay Grant
'Thelma' Stand-ins
Julie Strain, Cee Ozenne
'Louise' Stand-in
Deborah Stenard
Dialect Coach
Timothy Monich

Animal Trainer
Grisco's Animals
Aerial Co-ordinator
Robert 'Bobby Z' Zajonc
Helicopter Pilots
David Paris, Don Hildebrand
Ground Safety
Cynthia V. Zajonc
Unit Publicist
Joe Everett

Cast
Susan Sarandon
Louise Sawyer
Geena Davis
Thelma Dickinson
Harvey Keitel
Hal Slocombe
Michael Madsen
Jimmy
Christopher McDonald
Darryl
Stephen Tobolowsky
Max
Brad Pitt
J.D.
Timothy Carhart
Harlan
Lucinda Jenney
Lena, the waitress
Jason Beghe
state trooper
Marco St. John
truck driver
Sonny Carl Davis
Albert
Ken Swofford
major
Shelly De Sai
East Indian motel clerk

Carol Mansell
waitress
Stephen Polk
surveillance man
Rob Roy Fitzgerald
plainclothes cop
Jack Lindine
I.D. tech
Michael Delman
Silver Bullet dancer
Kristel L. Rose
girl smoker
Noel Walcott
mountain bike rider

11,643 feet
129 minutes

Dolby stereo SR
Colour by
DeLuxe
Anamorphic [Panavision]

Also Published

L'Argent
Kent Jones (1999)

Blade Runner
Scott Bukatman (1997)

Blue Velvet
Michael Atkinson (1997)

Caravaggio
Leo Bersani & Ulysse Dutoit
(1999)

Crash
Iain Sinclair (1999)

The Crying Game
Jane Giles (1997)

Dead Man
Jonathan Rosenbaum
(2000)

Don't Look Now
Mark Sanderson (1996)

Easy Rider
Lee Hill (1996)

The Exorcist
Mark Kermode (1997,
2nd edn 1998)

Independence Day
Michael Rogin (1998)

Last Tango in Paris
David Thompson (1998)

**Once Upon a Time in
America**
Adrian Martin (1998)

Pulp Fiction
Dana Polan (2000)

**Salo or The 120 Days of
Sodom**
Gary Indiana (2000)

Seven
Richard Dyer (1999)

The Terminator
Sean French (1996)

The Thing
Anne Billson (1997)

**The 'Three Colours'
Trilogy**
Geoff Andrew (1998)

The Right Stuff
Tom Charity (1997)

The Wings of the Dove
Robin Wood (1999)

Titanic
David M. Lubin (1999)

**Women on the Verge of a
Nervous Breakdown**
Peter William Evans (1996)

**WR – Mysteries of the
Organism**
Raymond Durgnat (1999)

Forthcoming

Do the Right Thing
Ed Guerrero (2001)

Star Wars
Peter Wollen (2001)